Increasing Your Peace: Anger Managem(

MW01702754

YOUR PROOF OF COURSE COMPLETION

Dear Student, *Today's date:*___________________________

Before you turn in this completed course book, please fill out this PROOF OF COURSE COMPLETION and get it signed and dated. Once completed, gently tear out this page and keep for your records. This will be your documentation that you have done your part. Having your proof of course completion signed and in your possession may come in handy if something happens and your completion is not recorded in your corrections file.

ME

My last name: ___________________________

My first name: ___________________________

My ID number: ___________________________

My housing: ___________________________

The name of the institution where I turned in my completed work:

____

PEER

The name of my Peer Mentor, or have your cellie or friend witness that they saw you doing your coursework: ___________________________
print clearly

Their ID number and housing is: ___________________________

____

Peer sign here:___________________________Date: ___________________________

STAFF

The staff or GOGI representative who received my work is:

____
print clearly

Staff or GOGI representative who received this workbook please sign here:

___________________________Date: ___________________________

Please tear out this page and retain for your records.

GOGI EDU
EDUCATION DIVISION
A Division of Getting Out by Going In

Increasing Your Peace: Anger Management The GOGI Way

Published by: GOGI Education
A division of Getting Out by Going In (GOGI)

This course is one of many GOGI In-Cell learning opportunities. This particular course is designed for you to read and write for one hour each day. By the time you complete this course, you will have invested forty hours of your time learning how to use the GOGI Tools.

With forty hours of consistent daily study, we are confident you will complete this course with increased levels of confidence regarding your ability to *Increase Your Peace* - the GOGI Way!

GOGI needs these books to be purchased.
Please do not make copies of this book. Making copies of this book is dishonest, and does not help GOGI expand and grow to serve all prisoners. GOGI offers many free materials and services, however if copies of this composition book are made we cannot sustain ourselves and fewer people will have access to GOGI.
Please check our website for donor-assistance, multiple discounts, and bulk order pricing of this and all GOGI certificate programs.

GOGI EDU is a division of the nonprofit, Getting Out by Going In (GOGI)

ISBN: 978-0-9972875-8-5

First edition, March 2016
Second edition, May 2017

This book is another in the family of GOGI materials such as:
Workshops, DVDs, curricula, educational media, and self-study materials designed to promote the GOGI Culture and teach the GOGI TOOLS FOR POSITIVE DECISION-MAKING.

THIS BOOK BELONGS TO:

Student Last Name: ______________________ Student First Name: ______________________

ID number: ______________________ Housing: ______________________

Prison name: ____

Prison address: ____

____

City: ______________________ State: __________ Zip: __________

Date you received this course: ______________________ Date of completion: ______________________

PRISON PURCHASE: If your prison purchased this course for you, it will be necessary to turn your completed coursebook in to the designated GOGI representative or staff in your prison, if you want credit for course completion.

FAMILY AND FRIENDS: If you or your family or friends paid $50.00 directly to GOGI and you received this course through the mail, then you will need to send your completed course book back to GOGI at the address below. GOGI academic staff will review the completed coursebook and you will receive your certificate through the mail.

IF YOU TRANSFER: If your prison purchased this course and you transferred or were released before completion, you will need to mail your completed course back to GOGI at the address below. GOGI academic staff will review the completed coursebook and you will receive your certificate through the mail. Please make certain to provide the address where you began the work and your current address.

HOW DID YOU RECEIVE THIS COURSE?

- ☐ Family/friend purchase
- ☐ Prison gave it to me
- ☐ I purchased with my funds
- ☐ It was given to me by a prisoner

Adopting the GOGI Way of Life has been the best choice I have ever made. In the interconnected web we live in our choices affect all. My community through Positive Actions is positive and supportive of healing and helping. The energy, worth, and value I have is limitless. I have found my purpose in life.

— GOGI - 4 - LIFE —

JASON YATES - GOGI LEADER

How Goofy is

When you live life with the GOGI Tools to guide you, life can be a lot of fun. Students of GOGI have fun. Learning is fun, especially when you learn The GOGI Way!

Your GOGI?

INCREASING MY PEACE – ACCOUNTABILITY BOX

DO YOU WANT CREDIT FOR THIS COURSE? REMEMBER TO KEEP TRACK OF YOUR DAILY STUDY BY COMPLETING THE INFORMATION BELOW TO GET YOUR CREDIT.

The month is________________; The day is ______________; The year is________; Solo study or group? ____________

INTRODUCTION TO THIS ANGER MANAGEMENT COURSE

By Coach Taylor, Founder/Lead Volunteer

For many years there has been great effort to help people "manage" their anger. There are 'Anger Management' courses, anger classes, anger books, anger audio files. There are weekend workshops, retreats, and training. They all seem to help people manage their anger, a little bit. But is "managing" your anger really your goal? Do you really want to be a better manager of anger?

Wouldn't it be more effective to teach you how to respond and react to life's inevitable difficulties in a manner that did not include anger?

WHAT IF anger were merely a "choice" you could make and, WHAT IF there were other choices, too? Choices like increasing your internal peace and not permitting things or people to disturb your journey towards being the best person you can possibly become.

This GOGI Course will supply you with a new and fresh perspective on "Anger Management" and provide you with keen insights into your right to choose anger if you want anger, and to choose internal peace if you want internal peace.

In this 'Anger Management' course, you will be able learn simple tools to select a response other than anger. You will be able to create alternatives for yourself that empower you beyond a temper tantrum. You will understand that you are fully capable and may manage, tend to, babysit, and care for your anger with these tools. Giving you powerful and positive choices is the outcome of this course.

We call this course INCREASING THE PEACE, and it is GOGI's alternative to traditional Anger Management classes that might not work as well as you would like. Since 2002, GOGI has listened to people in prisons and jails.

Our courses are developed with intense respect for the journey of our students. Collectively, the GOGI students have stated that Anger Management courses could be much more effective if the GOGI Tools were taught with the other information related to anger and its illusion of power over individuals.

So, we have created this course. And, I have great confidence that through this course you will learn and practice many things. Most importantly, rather than "manage" your anger, we want you to increase the levels of peace you feel inside you so much that there is no room for anger to bubble up.

Let's get going. Let's start INCREASING YOUR PEACE.

With Love,

Coach

Coach Taylor
Founder/Lead Volunteer

The Faces of GOGI Graduates

Your Face Belongs Here!

INCREASING MY PEACE – ACCOUNTABILITY BOX

DO YOU WANT CREDIT FOR THIS COURSE? REMEMBER TO KEEP TRACK OF YOUR DAILY STUDY BY COMPLETING THE INFORMATION BELOW TO GET YOUR CREDIT.

The month is________________; The day is _______________; The year is________; Solo study or group? ____________

WELCOME

Welcome to one of the many GOGI courses offered to people who are interested in making more positive decisions in their lives. This particular course is an eight-week course designed to increase your skills through reading and writing for 30 to 45 minutes each day.

This is course is part of a series of GOGI in-cell courses designed to help prepare you for success. This specific course will help you increase your level of peace and reduce the emotions of anger. You may find the other courses help you apply the GOGI Tools to other aspects of your life, permitting you to see ways to increase your peace in the future, the present, and even in your thoughts of the past.

This photo shows a group of GOGI students at a California State Prison.

IF YOU INVEST YOUR TIME...

Of course, you are wise enough to know that in eight weeks you will not magically change everything about your anger or frustration. If you invest your time into this course, and if you use the tools of this course, you will have the ability to make more positive decisions. Making more positive decisions for eight weeks is great. Making those same positive decisions for an additional 12, 24, 48, and 52 weeks is even more powerful. Practicing these tools, and using them may be tough, but it can be your goal.

In this course you will learn simple tools for increasing your level of internal peace. At GOGI, we have come to understand that when you increase your level of peace, there is less room for the unpleasant feelings of anger.

When we say GOGI-4-Life, we mean you can create the best life possible – with GOGI!

This photo shows Coach Tevita Niu who has since been released from prison and now is a GOGI Coach – on the outside. Coach Tevita volunteers his time to anyone and EVERYONE sharing the tools that helped him find his freedom.

> *Anger is a choice, but it is not your only choice. You have unlimited ways to respond to life's inevitable challenges. With GOGI your options increase. Increasing your peace happens when you increase your GOGI.*
>
> Coach

INCREASING MY PEACE – ACCOUNTABILITY BOX

DO YOU WANT CREDIT FOR THIS COURSE? REMEMBER TO KEEP TRACK OF YOUR DAILY STUDY BY COMPLETING THE INFORMATION BELOW TO GET YOUR CREDIT.

The month is________________; The day is ______________; The year is________; Solo study or group? ____________

THE GOGI COURSES ARE FOR EVERYONE

Each of the GOGI Courses are specifically designed to be used in a wide variety of learning and study settings. The GOGI Courses may be issued as a self-study course provided to you by an educator or case manager. The GOGI courses may also be used as text material for small study groups supervised by an educator or case manager. Teachers may also find these courses helpful in empowering students with the tools they need to make positive decisions.

In this photo, formerly incarcerated and never-been incarcerated GOGI volunteers hold up the stamps that prisoners send into the GOGI mailroom to help our outreach efforts to spread GOGI across the globe. Prisoners are GOGI's greatest number of donors, by the way!

The GOGI Courses are also used in programming and therapeutic community environments, mental health environments, transitional settings, and settings of incarceration or as an alternative to incarceration.

The GOGI Courses are also available to students who wish to engage in independent GOGI correspondence course study directly supervised by GOGI educators.

The educational division of GOGI offers a variety of self-improvement courses to many Departments of Correction who in turn offer rehabilitative education to prisoners. We also offer courses and programming to educational and mental health organizations.

The GOGI Courses are also offered as court mandated alternatives to incarceration, and as outpatient study materials, as well as to individuals seeking correspondence course opportunities.

MATERIALS AVAILABLE TO EVERYONE

The GOGI Course materials are available for purchase by any organization or individual. If you received this course from someone else, or prison or a jail, they have purchased it for you. If you ordered it yourself, it means you used your money and purchased the course by sending in payment and receiving the course from the publisher.

If you received this course as a gift from family or friends, it means they ordered the course from GOGI at our online store and had it shipped directly to you from the publisher.

GOGI offers discounted, donor-supported, and bulk order pricing for multiple copies. Learn more about GOGI's courses online at www.gettingoutbygoingin.org or by writing:
GOGI EDUCATION DIVISION, PO Box 2274, Mesquite, Nevada 89024.

This art is a gift to GOGI from GOGI Charlie H.

INCREASING MY PEACE – ACCOUNTABILITY BOX

DO YOU WANT CREDIT FOR THIS COURSE? REMEMBER TO KEEP TRACK OF YOUR DAILY STUDY BY COMPLETING THE INFORMATION BELOW TO GET YOUR CREDIT.

The month is_______________; The day is ______________; The year is________; Solo study or group? ____________

OUR GOGI HISTORY

GOGI was given its name by prisoners at The Federal Correctional Institution, Terminal Island, outside of San Pedro, California. The men who participated in GOGI Groups from 2002-2004 contributed to the creation of GOGI's name, as well as the title of "Coach" for the facilitators, and the "Tools" to help them act on proven psychological, cognitive, and behavioral methodologies for change. Six tools were created by men at Terminal Island.

*When you read that GOGI was created by prisoners at the Federal Prison called Terminal Island in San Pedro, California, what do you think?*____________________________________

More than 350 women who were housed in the GOGI Campus at the Los Angeles County Jail from 2007 - 2009 contributed to the final set of tools which now make up the totality of the GOGI TOOLS FOR POSITIVE DECISION-MAKING. They created the pledge, the meeting format, the first set of GOGI poems/art pieces/dances/songs/and children's rhymes.

When you read that six of the GOGI Tools were created by women in jail, and they created the GOGI pledge and meeting format, what do you think? ________________________________

____

As GOGI expanded across the nation from 2002 to today, prisoners from nearly every part of the country in Federal, State, and County settings of incarceration contributed to the advancement of GOGI as a POSITIVE PRISON CULTURE. Many of those people were released and have taken GOGI home to their families and communities.

What do you think about GOGI being seen as a "POSITIVE CULTURE" and not just a program?

____

____

____

GOGI is grateful to any prisoner brave enough to make lasting changes in their DECISION-MAKING. We know it is not easy and we want you to know you are not alone in this journey. Thank you for being a part of the solution.

*What do you think when you read that you are not alone in your GOGI studies?*______________

____

What does that mean to you? ____

____

What do you think about being part of a solution rather than part of the problem? ____________

____

____

INCREASING MY PEACE – ACCOUNTABILITY BOX

DO YOU WANT CREDIT FOR THIS COURSE? REMEMBER TO KEEP TRACK OF YOUR DAILY STUDY BY COMPLETING THE INFORMATION BELOW TO GET YOUR CREDIT.

The month is________________; The day is ________________; The year is__________; Solo study or group? ____________

DO I have reason to be ANGRY ? -4- SURE ! but, Should I allow my ANGER to CONTROL ME ? ABSOLUTELY NOT ! YET MOST of MY LIFE that's exactly what I did; being impulsive and reacting to the slightest of slights ended-up causing me to hit under rock bottom and at some-point I ended-up asking MYSELF :

• WHERE DO I REALLY WANT TO BE ? • HOW DO I REALLY WANT TO BE CARRIED ?

NO-MATTER how bad it is, it can get worse ! But, NO-matter HOW BAD it is, it CAN CAN get BETTER !

PEOPLE, You don't have to hit bottom like I did, You don't have to be where I've been AND I've been to some dark Places, both Physically and mentally... IF your tired of allowing your emotions = (FEELINGS) to make your decisions, IF you're tired of fighting a never ending battle of strife and you would rather enjoy some Peace and Prosperity ? Then it's time to come-up with a Postive battle Plan, one that teaches about the SPACE of your BODY and MIND functioning as a UNIT. At this Point I hope Your WONDERING – "HOW DO I DO THAT !?!" GOGI TOOL'S

GOGI TOOL'S -R- NEW INPUT DATA -4- YOU TO MANAGE Your ANGER-ANXIETY-STRESS- AND TENSION = (NEGATIVE DATA) GOGI Tools allow YOU to shift Negative data by replacing The SPACE they TAKE-UP with (Positive DATA) that You can use in Your decision making Process. GOGI IN Short is Positive DATA skill sets that are broke down into -4- simple Yet highly effective sections that allow you to use Your body as a TOOL connected with your mind focusing in on the (3P's) POSITIVE - PRODUCTIVE-AND POWERFUL – (3P's) which -R- choice tools that will develop THE DATA OF YOUR minds (-TWA-) THOUGHTS- WORDS- AND ACTIONS (-TWA-) by building your energy in a FORWARD momentum in your thinking which in-turn begins Creating FREEDOM of SERVICE for Yourself and surroundings.

HERE'S A BREAKDOWN OF HOW THE GOGI TOOL'S WORK

B.O.M.B = BOSS OF MY BRAIN is done as a simple Yet complex understanding OF how your BRAIN ACTUALLY works AND lets You know that You-R-control of Your THOUGHTS- WORDS - AND ACTIONS by 1st realizing where you're at in your HEAD : AM I IN MY HABITS - EMOTIONS - or IN the - SMART PARTS of my BRAINS PROCESSING ?.. YOU CAN ACTIVATE The SMART PART OF your BRAIN by

BELLY BREATHING = belly breathing is a tool that instantly relaxes your entire Person because your blood begins flowing correctly throughout your body which then gives you an energetic reaction to FLIP THE

5 SECOND LIGHT-SWITCH five second light-switch is a a moment to reflect on (POSITIVE DATA) TO SWAP OUT OVER NEGATIVE DATA. IMPULSES -R- DATA TRIGGERS THAT YOU HAVE THE POWER TO control. YOUR BODY AND THOUGHTS -R- SPACE DATA. that can be MENTALLY Shifted INTO A DESirable CHANGE

ONCE YOU IDENTIFY – Acknowledge SAID DATA TRIGGERS and begin USING GOGI'S Positive decision making tools in Your (T-W-A) with the (3P'S) of choice YOU BEGIN USING MOVING FOWARD TOOLS :

FORGIVE =, FOR me to GIVE Productively, I must remove negative data from harming me in any manner. I have to unhook from Negative DATA with

LET GO = let go of negative data by visualizing any SAid negative Data, harming my Productivity, in my hand and squash it and toss it behind me so I can claim responsbility of any said situation.

CLAIM Responsibility Claiming responsibility isn't saying it's my fault but what it is saying is that I'm strong enough to make a decision I'm proud about That developes a creativity that begans a WHAT IF STATEMENT...

INCREASING MY PEACE – ACCOUNTABILITY BOX

DO YOU WANT CREDIT FOR THIS COURSE? REMEMBER TO KEEP TRACK OF YOUR DAILY STUDY BY COMPLETING THE INFORMATION BELOW TO GET YOUR CREDIT.

The month is__________________; The day is ________________; The year is________; Solo study or group? ______________

WHAT IF - What if- I'm not Past - what if- I'm not going to allow negative DATA TO DEFINE who I am or where I'm HEADED?!

REALITY CHECK Realit[y] Check is A FACT check, a truth that I'M MORTAL, I'M HUMAN so I will MAKE Mistakes. This is how I learn. so when I do make a mistake = Focus on THE Forward steps I took to get me to this Poin[t] and take these backwards steps As a learning curve so that I can use this Mistake as a moment to benefit rather than beating myself up

These GOGI TOOL'S ARE A service of FREEDOM THAT ARE ULTIMATE FREEDOM is an experiance of no matter where you are That you choose to be of service to others which allows you to live ultimate Free being GOGI...

PEER COACH, Justin Allee

Just Cause

This art is a gift to GOGI from Ray.

INCREASING MY PEACE – ACCOUNTABILITY BOX

DO YOU WANT CREDIT FOR THIS COURSE? REMEMBER TO KEEP TRACK OF YOUR DAILY STUDY BY COMPLETING THE INFORMATION BELOW TO GET YOUR CREDIT.

The month is________________; The day is ______________; The year is________; Solo study or group? ____________

FREQUENTLY ASKED QUESTIONS

I like working with others. Can I use this in a group study setting?

Why not? If you have a group and you can use this material to inspire the possibility of change for many individuals, that is great. You can also use this book for a book club, book reports, or to supplement GOGI Group study, your independent study, or for readings during presentations about GOGI. You can even use these questions as a supplement to other texts and studies. If the goal is to help you make more positive decisions in your daily life, then the more ways you can use this material the better off you will be, the stronger you will be, and the more confident you will be. Since you are the boss of your self-improvement, you can be creative in the different ways you use the material in this book.

What do you think of the above? ____

____

____

I flipped through the pages and some of these questions seem a bit too personal. What if I don't want to answer some of them?

You are the boss of your journey in completing this course. You know that what you write is only as private as your situation may permit. The questions will not require you to reveal more than you are comfortable writing. There is no need to give details of anything that makes you feel uncomfortable or places you in jeopardy. You can learn and grow without getting into details about harm you suffered or harm you caused. Simply reading the questions will cause you to consider them within the deepest part of you, even if you do not write what you are thinking and feeling. This course truly is more about who you are today and what you can do today so you can write about those things. If something seems a bit too personal, you can modify the question and answer according to your comfort level. Remember, you are the boss of this course. As long as it is completed and you have done the writing that addresses the topic, you will have completed the course. We want you to be comfortable and not feel pressured to go beyond your level of comfort or safety.

What do you think of the above? ____

____

Who came up with this course?

Please do not forget that GOGI was designed by prisoners for other prisoners. Every tool you will learn was designed, named, and developed by prisoners. If you think the name Getting Out by Going In and the nickname "GOGI" sound funny, you can blame a prisoner. They named GOGI. Even the questions in this book were presented, reviewed, written, and approved by prisoners.

What do you think of the above?____

____

DO YOU WANT CREDIT FOR THIS COURSE? REMEMBER TO KEEP TRACK OF YOUR DAILY STUDY BY COMPLETING THE INFORMATION BELOW TO GET YOUR CREDIT.

The month is________________; The day is ______________; The year is________; Solo study or group? __________

But courses just don't work for me. Ever.

If in the past you used the excuse that courses or lessons or books did not quite ring true to your own life, you won't have that excuse with GOGI. That is because GOGI is the voice of the prisoners who have emerged out of the hopelessness and who are now dedicated to helping you find your way out, too. If this course does not work to help you create a better life for yourself, maybe it is time for you to look at yourself in the mirror and think about who it is that is standing in your way of success. Are you prepared to be the best boss possible? We will see.

What do you think of the above? ____

____

____

My friend heard about GOGI when he was in a county jail in some state I didn't even know existed. Is GOGI everywhere?

It is common to find people who have studied GOGI in other facilities. As of 2017, more than 37 states have GOGI students. GOGI grows organically and virally, through prisoner word of mouth and, it won't be long until we reach our goal of 250,000 active GOGI students. When we reach that number, we will have the backing of enough people to begin creating GOGI groups in every prison and jail. There will be GOGI Campuses where our leaders can be trained to be of service to the incarcerated and released offenders, and GOGI facilities where only those who are serious about change can do their time. Yes, GOGI is everywhere and GOGI will still be on this earth in the year 2300 as a peaceful, powerful, and productive way to unite all people into the world of internal freedom through service.

What do you think of the above? ____

____

____

What is GOGI?

GOGI is the voice of the prisoners who are dedicated to making positive changes in their lives. All prisoners...all races...all religions...all sizes and shapes, all colors and cultures. GOGI is for every living human being and offers simple tools which were designed and delivered by prisoners for other prisoners to make their lives better. GOGI has emerged as an alternative to a violent prison culture. GOGI is a positive culture, which promotes positive leadership and healing of communities from the inside out.

What do you think of the above? ____

____

____

____

INCREASING MY PEACE – ACCOUNTABILITY BOX

DO YOU WANT CREDIT FOR THIS COURSE? REMEMBER TO KEEP TRACK OF YOUR DAILY STUDY BY COMPLETING THE INFORMATION BELOW TO GET YOUR CREDIT.

The month is________________; The day is _______________; The year is________; Solo study or group? ___________

But I go to church. Is this against my religion?

If your religion states you do not need to make positive decisions, then GOGI might not be for you. If your religion wants you to make more positive decision, it is likely GOGI can help you. If your religion states that you cannot learn with other humans who want to make positive decisions, then GOGI might not be for you. If your religion does not want you to be of service to mankind and does not want you to be a humble servant offering help to others, then GOGI might not be for you. If your religious leader objects to GOGI studies, you may offer to let them review the materials to make sure it is not against the religious teachings you follow. We have not yet found a religion that prohibits GOGI studies. We have found religious leaders who, once they review the materials, become supportive of their congregation learning tools to help them make more positive decisions. GOGI offers simple decision-making tools for all humans. Anyone who ever has made a bad decision can benefit from learning how to make more positive decisions. Positive decision-making does not belong to any one culture nor does it belong to any one religion. All humans can make more positive decisions and the GOGI Tools are for all humans.

We DO know, however, that people who practice a formal religion usually are better in their practice when they use GOGI Tools. We have been told for more than a decade by Christians that learning GOGI Tools helps them become better Christians. Similarly, Muslim prisoners have told us that the GOGI Tools are consistent with their teachings and makes them a better Muslim. Students of Judaism, Jehovah's Witness, Hindus, Primal-indigenous, American Indian, Rosicrucian, Orthodox, and every other possible religious and spiritual study can be improved upon when the human being learns how to make more positive decisions.

What do you think of the above? ____

____

____

____

I go to AA is this the same thing?

Any positive and prosocial association is going to help you strengthen your ability to remain strong. We have heard of AA groups referring to the GOGI Tools when someone stands up and voices a struggle with addiction. "Use your BELLY BREATHING," was once shouted from the audience, which caused a bit of laughter among the meeting attendees. Use of the GOGI materials is appropriate in settings where people are learning how to make more positive decisions. GOGI is not a replacement for anything. GOGI is intended as an ADDITIONAL reinforcement. Keep going to AA. Keep going to church. Keep attending any and all classes to expand your mind. And keep your GOGI Tools in your pocket so you can do a better job at all your activities.

What do you think of the above? ____

____

____

DO YOU WANT CREDIT FOR THIS COURSE? REMEMBER TO KEEP TRACK OF YOUR DAILY STUDY BY COMPLETING THE INFORMATION BELOW TO GET YOUR CREDIT.

The month is________________; The day is ______________; The year is________; Solo study or group? ____________

GOGI works because it is the voice of the prisoner. Up until now, there has been a top-down approach to helping people in prisons and jails. With GOGI, we build the individual from the ground up, from the inside out. And that is how all systems experience lasting change: from the inside out.

What do you think of the above? ____

____

Is there proof that GOGI works?

GOGI combines the experience of the prisoner with proven psychological concepts for human change. In the development of GOGI it was the voice of the prisoner that was more important than the scientific studies into the efficacy of a treatment modality. (Basically, we didn't want anyone who believes in a top-down approach to meddle in the creation of GOGI.) We wanted the prisoners to discover how change happened FOR THEM. From the inside out. Without top-down direction. Sometimes institutions need "evidence" that a "program" works before they let our students conduct GOGI meetings. For their convenience we have assembled the proof of the psychological modalities used in each and every GOGI Tool. We send out this article when we receive inquires by corrections staff asking for anything to support their request to permit GOGI to expand. We have the evidence departments of corrections needs to justify giving permission for GOGI to grow. But we prefer to let the GOGI student be the evidence and let the proof be in the reduction of incident reports in a GOGI dorm. We prefer to have staff notice, and report, that GOGI students are more manageable, respectful, and trustworthy. We prefer to let the GOGI graduates return successfully to their community and only go back to prison as a guest speaker in, and out, of the FRONT door. At GOGI our proof is in the way we choose to respond and react to any and all situations.

What do you think of the above? ____

____

____

____

____

____

Is that it?

Is that all you need to know about GOGI? Not by a long shot, but it is enough for you to be successful in this course. By the end of this course, you may have more questions. That will be the time you request another GOGI book where you will find more answers.

What do you think of the above? ____

____

____

INCREASING MY PEACE – ACCOUNTABILITY BOX

DO YOU WANT CREDIT FOR THIS COURSE? REMEMBER TO KEEP TRACK OF YOUR DAILY STUDY BY COMPLETING THE INFORMATION BELOW TO GET YOUR CREDIT.

The month is__________________; The day is ________________; The year is_________; Solo study or group? ____________

THE GOGI COURSE
INCREASING YOUR PEACE: ANGER MANAGEMENT - THE GOGI WAY
COURSE OBJECTIVES AND SYLLABUS

The academic objective of this course:

The objective of this course is to provide you with simple tools for positive decision-making that lead to control of anger. This course is designed to help you improve your ability to replace anger by providing you with decision-making tools others have found very helpful.

You will be able to use these tools as options to prevent yourself (or others) from causing anger within you. You will be provided with an ability to create alternatives to anger. These are concrete options for you when life deals out its inevitable challenges and you are tempted to resort to anger as a response. In your own words, what would you say are YOUR objectives in taking this course?

What would YOU like to achieve? ____

____

The syllabus/schedule of this course:

You are to complete one page of reading and writing each day. By the end of your eight-weeks, you will have completed your entire course. Your course may be done entirely on your own, or may be included in group study or classroom study. As long as you are doing one page each day, you are doing exactly what is required.

In your own words, what is expected of you each day? ______________________________

____

____

Your course will have a different subject each week. Below are your weekly subjects:

Week One:	INCREASING YOUR PEACE WITH BOSS OF MY BRAIN
Week Two:	INCREASING YOUR PEACE WITH BELLY BREATHING
Week Three:	INCREASING YOUR PEACE WITH FIVE SECOND LIGHTSWITCH
Week Four:	PLANNING YOUR REACTIONS
Week Five	PLANNING YOUR FUTURE USING TOOLS OF THE BODY
Week Six:	INCREASING YOUR PEACE BY USING TOOLS OF THE BODY
Week Seven:	INCREASING YOUR PEACE APPLYING YOUR NEW TOOLS
Week Eight:	INCREASING YOUR PEACE AND MOVING FORWARD WITH YOUR LIFE

What GOGI Tools will you study in weeks one and two? ______________________________

____

INCREASING MY PEACE – ACCOUNTABILITY BOX

DO YOU WANT CREDIT FOR THIS COURSE? REMEMBER TO KEEP TRACK OF YOUR DAILY STUDY BY COMPLETING THE INFORMATION BELOW TO GET YOUR CREDIT.

The month is________________; The day is ______________; The year is________; Solo study or group? _____________

When you read that you will be putting your tools into practice, what do you think that means?

____

____

*Do you think changes in your life will require practice? (a "yes" or "no" is fine here)*____________

Have you heard of or read anything about the GOGI Tools prior to taking this course? Briefly explain any previous learning or knowledge you have of GOGI and the tools. ______________________

____

____

____

What we expect from you:

To do your GOGI studies and get the most out of them, there are a few things you will need to do. Below is a list to guide you in doing your very best work.

- Of course, you must do your own writing. If you do not know how to write, please get permission from GOGI or staff for someone to write for you.
- Please be more creative than one word answers. "Yes" or "No" are not adequate responses to the questions. We know you can do better than that.
- Each question may have two to three lines for you to write. Do your best to fill all the lines and if you need more space, please feel free to write on additional paper.
- If a question is too personal, you can respond to that question in a way that does not make you uncomfortable. Change the question to fit your level of comfort.
- At the end of your course, you will turn in your workbook. But just because your course is over, please don't stop your GOGI studies. At GOGI, we want you to be "GOGI-4-Life." All you will need to do is consistently practice your tools and share them with others.

*Do you understand all the above requirements? (a "yes" or "no" is fine here)*______________

Do you think you will have any challenges too big for you to complete this course? ____________

____

____

*What might be ways you can overcome any challenge so you are successful in the completion of the course?*____

____

____

INCREASING MY PEACE – ACCOUNTABILITY BOX

DO YOU WANT CREDIT FOR THIS COURSE? REMEMBER TO KEEP TRACK OF YOUR DAILY STUDY BY COMPLETING THE INFORMATION BELOW TO GET YOUR CREDIT.

The month is__________________; The day is __________________; The year is__________; Solo study or group? ______________

While this course is not designed for the student to study according to the GOGI Calendar, all GOGI Group study occurs according to the GOGI national Calendar. While doing this course, you will learn about the calendar, but will not study according to the calendar until you begin group or independent study.

The GOGI Calendar

Week 1 begins on the first Monday of each month.

JANUARY

Week 1 BOSS OF MY BRAIN
Week 2 BELLY BREATHING
Week 3 FIVE SECOND LIGHTSWITCH
Week 4 POSITIVE THOUGHTS

FEBRUARY

Week 1 POSITIVE WORDS
Week 2 POSITIVE ACTIONS
Week 3 CLAIM RESPONSIBILITY
Week 4 LET GO

MARCH

Week 1 FOR-GIVE
Week 2 WHAT IF
Week 3 REALITY CHECK
Week 4 ULTIMATE FREEDOM

APRIL

Week 1 BOSS OF MY BRAIN
Week 2 BELLY BREATHING
Week 3 FIVE SECOND LIGHTSWITCH
Week 4 POSITIVE THOUGHTS

MAY

Week 1 POSITIVE WORDS
Week 2 POSITIVE ACTIONS
Week 3 CLAIM RESPONSIBILITY
Week 4 LET GO

JUNE

Week 1 FOR-GIVE
Week 2 WHAT IF
Week 3 REALITY CHECK
Week 4 ULTIMATE FREEDOM

JULY

Week 1 BOSS OF MY BRAIN
Week 2 BELLY BREATHING
Week 3 FIVE SECOND LIGHTSWITCH
Week 4 POSITIVE THOUGHTS

AUGUST

Week 1 POSITIVE WORDS
Week 2 POSITIVE ACTIONS
Week 3 CLAIM RESPONSIBILITY
Week 4 LET GO

SEPTEMBER

Week 1 FOR-GIVE
Week 2 WHAT IF
Week 3 REALITY CHECK
Week 4 ULTIMATE FREEDOM

OCTOBER

Week 1 BOSS OF MY BRAIN
Week 2 BELLY BREATHING
Week 3 FIVE SECOND LIGHTSWITCH
Week 4 POSITIVE THOUGHTS

NOVEMBER

Week 1 POSITIVE WORDS
Week 2 POSITIVE ACTIONS
Week 3 CLAIM RESPONSIBILITY
Week 4 LET GO

DECEMBER

Week 1 FOR-GIVE
Week 2 WHAT IF
Week 3 REALITY CHECK
Week 4 ULTIMATE FREEDOM

**Whenever there is a fifth Monday in the month, review all four sections of Tools.*

INCREASING MY PEACE – ACCOUNTABILITY BOX

DO YOU WANT CREDIT FOR THIS COURSE? REMEMBER TO KEEP TRACK OF YOUR DAILY STUDY BY COMPLETING THE INFORMATION BELOW TO GET YOUR CREDIT.

The month is________________; The day is ________________; The year is________; Solo study or group? ________________

The GOGI Tools

Before you get started with Week One of INCREASING YOUR PEACE, take some time to read the following pages which are a brief introduction to the GOGI TOOLS FOR POSITIVE DECISION-MAKING.

The Tools are broken into four sections:

These are the tools you will learn in this course.

TOOLS OF THE BODY

- BOSS OF MY BRAIN
- BELLY BREATHING
- FIVE SECOND LIGHTSWITCH

TOOLS OF CHOICE

- POSITIVE THOUGHTS
- POSITIVE WORDS
- POSITIVE ACTIONS

TOOLS OF MOVING FORWARD

- CLAIM RESPONSIBILITY
- LET GO
- FOR-GIVE

TOOLS OF CREATION

- WHAT IF
- REALITY CHECK
- ULTIMATE FREEDOM

Understanding the GOGI Tools:

Each tool has KEYWORDS, a STATEMENT OF PURPOSE AND OWNERSHIP, an OBJECTIVE, a TOOL INTRO, and tips on HOW TO USE the tool. These sections will help you to understand the basics of the GOGI Tools.

The GOGI Calendar:

Around the globe, no matter where you are, when you study according to the GOGI Calendar, you will never be alone in your GOGI studies. It is MORE IMPORTANT to be on the Calendar than to start GOGI studies with a particular tool.

GOGI Tool

MY GOGI TOOL BOSS OF MY BRAIN

The weeks to study BOSS OF MY BRAIN are:

1st Week of January
1st Week of April
1st Week of July
1st Week of October

KEYWORDS – BOSS OF MY BRAIN

THE THREE PARTS: There are three parts that matter: SMART PART, EMOTIONAL PART, and the OLD HABIT PART. Which one is the boss right now?

STATEMENT OF PURPOSE AND OWNERSHIP – BOSS OF MY BRAIN

I am BOSS OF MY BRAIN and I have complete control over each thought I create. Because I am BOSS OF MY BRAIN, I can change my thoughts at any time. No one has control over my thoughts because only I am the BOSS OF MY BRAIN.

OBJECTIVE – BOSS OF MY BRAIN

Your goal with this week's tool is to learn that you have a choice in how your brain thinks. You can SMART think, EMOTIONAL think, or you can OLD HABIT think. You are the boss of how you think and you will learn how to be the boss with this week's tool called BOSS OF MY BRAIN.

TOOL INTRO – BOSS OF MY BRAIN

Did you know that GOGI believes there are only three parts of your brain you need to understand? At GOGI we focus on these three parts of your brain:

- The SMART PART
- The EMOTIONAL PART
- The OLD HABIT PART

HOW TO USE – BOSS OF MY BRAIN

If you want to use the GOGI TOOL called BOSS OF MY BRAIN, all you need to do is ask yourself, "What part of my brain is in charge right now?" It's that simple.

- The **SMART PART** of your brain is where you learn new things. This is the part of the brain that will help you be strong and make positive decisions.
- The **EMOTIONAL PART** is filled with opinions, drama, anger, or hurt. When you let this part of your brain be the boss, you are not going to make positive decisions.
- The **OLD HABIT PART** of your brain is where all those old habits you no longer need are stored. The less you rely on old habits, the more room you will have for the SMART PART to help you create new positive habits.

MY GOGI TOOL BELLY BREATHING

The weeks to study BELLY BREATHING are:

2nd Week of January
2nd Week of April
2nd Week of July
2nd Week of October

KEYWORDS – BELLY BREATHING

ONE HAND ON MY CHEST, ONE HAND ON MY BELLY. WHICH ONE IS MOVING RIGHT NOW? My brain works better when my belly moves.

STATEMENT OF PURPOSE AND OWNERSHIP – BELLY BREATHING

With BELLY BREATHING I can instantly relax my body and I can make positive decisions. When I am BELLY BREATHING I take control of my thoughts and feelings.

OBJECTIVE – BELLY BREATHING

Your goal in learning this week's tool is to breathe with your chest remaining still and your belly moving in and out. This is your most powerful way to breathe and you can achieve this with this week's tool called BELLY BREATHING.

TOOL INTRO – BELLY BREATHING

Did you know that when you breathe with your belly it actually makes you smarter? It is true. This is because when you breathe into your belly you are also getting oxygen into your brain, and that makes the brain work better. GOGI believes there are two types of breathing: breathing with your chest, or BELLY BREATHING.

HOW TO USE – BELLY BREATHING

You can use the BELLY BREATHING tool at any time. Here are three ways to use the tool:

- You can actually put one hand on your chest and one hand on your stomach and see which one is moving.
- Or, just put one hand on your stomach to make sure it is moving.
- And, if you are breathing with your chest, you can direct the air all the way into your stomach area and begin BELLY BREATHING.

GOGI Tool

MY GOGI TOOL FIVE SECOND LIGHTSWITCH

The weeks to study FIVE SECOND LIGHTSWITCH are:

3rd Week of January
3rd Week of April
3rd Week of July
3rd Week of October

KEYWORDS – FIVE SECOND LIGHTSWITCH

OLD THOUGHT = NEW ACTION.
I have an OLD THOUGHT and I have a NEW ACTION.

STATEMENT OF PURPOSE AND OWNERSHIP – FIVE SECOND LIGHTSWITCH

I can flip my FIVE SECOND LIGHTSWITCH and instantly change any negative thought to a new action. There is no negative thought more powerful than my new action when I flip my FIVE SECOND LIGHTSWITCH.

OBJECTIVE – FIVE SECOND LIGHTSWITCH

Your goal this week is to build the new habit of choosing a new action every time you have an old negative thought. You can do this by using your FIVE SECOND LIGHTSWITCH, which is this week's tool.

TOOL INTRO – FIVE SECOND LIGHTSWITCH

Here is an example. When you are told, "just don't think about smoking a cigarette," it seems that all you can think about is the cigarette. When beginning to train your mind to create other thoughts, it is nearly impossible to think that you could simply stop thinking about something that consumed a lot of thinking for a long time.

That is why FIVE SECOND LIGHTSWITCH works; it realizes that your mind has been trained to head down a particular road, almost like autopilot. The GOGI Tool FIVE SECOND LIGHTSWITCH permits you to observe that thought, and then replace that thought with a new, more positive and productive action.

At GOGI we call this flipping the FIVE SECOND LIGHTSWITCH. This tool provides you with the power to reroute your brain activity so you are able to be stronger in your positive choices.

HOW TO USE – FIVE SECOND LIGHTSWITCH

You can use the FIVE SECOND LIGHTSWITCH tool when your thoughts seem to be the boss of you. When an urge seems really really strong, the FIVE SECOND LIGHTSWITCH is a powerful tool to use.

The key to FIVE SECOND LIGHTSWITCH is to have your replacement action ready. If you have your replacement action ready, you are likely to have great success with FIVE SECOND LIGHTSWITCH.

MY GOGI TOOL POSITIVE THOUGHTS

The weeks to study POSITIVE THOUGHTS are:

4th Week of January
4th Week of April
4th Week of July
4th Week of October

KEYWORDS – POSITIVE THOUGHTS

THE THREE P's
Is it POWERFUL?
Is it PRODUCTIVE?
Is it POSITIVE?

STATEMENT OF PURPOSE AND OWNERSHIP – POSITIVE THOUGHTS

My POSITIVE THOUGHTS set the direction of my life from this moment forward. I focus on POSITIVE THOUGHTS, even when it is difficult or challenging. No matter what is happening, I can create POSITIVE THOUGHTS.

OBJECTIVE – POSITIVE THOUGHTS

Your goal with this week's tool is to practice being the boss of your thinking and to choose thoughts that are POWERFUL, PRODUCTIVE, and POSITIVE. You will practice this with the tool POSITIVE THOUGHTS.

TOOL INTRO – POSITIVE THOUGHTS

You are the boss of your brain and you can create any thought you want to create. When you force your brain to create POSITIVE THOUGHTS you are actually using the tool POSITIVE THOUGHTS.

Your brain will follow your orders and if you use the tool POSITIVE THOUGHTS over and over again, eventually your brain will begin to create POSITIVE THOUGHTS on its own.

HOW TO USE – POSITIVE THOUGHTS

You can use POSITIVE THOUGHTS by considering your thoughts and asking yourself, "Is this thought POWERFUL? Is it PRODUCTIVE? Is it POSITIVE?"
When you ask yourself these three questions, you will become more in control of your thoughts.
THE THREE P'S

- Is it POWERFUL?
- Is it PRODUCTIVE?
- Is it POSITIVE?

If the answer is no, then pick a more POSITIVE THOUGHT.

GOGI Tool

MY GOGI TOOL POSITIVE WORDS

The weeks to study POSITIVE WORDS are:

1st Week of February
1st Week of May
1st Week of August
1st Week of November

KEYWORDS – POSITIVE WORDS

THE THREE P's
Is it POWERFUL?
Is it PRODUCTIVE?
Is it POSITIVE?

STATEMENT OF PURPOSE AND OWNERSHIP – POSITIVE WORDS

My POSITIVE WORDS tell the world what I am thinking and who I am today. I use POSITIVE WORDS to break free from my past and move forward into a positive future.

OBJECTIVE – POSITIVE WORDS

Your goal this week is to practice being the boss of the words you choose. You will choose words that are POWERFUL, PRODUCTIVE, and POSITIVE when you learn the tool POSITIVE WORDS.

TOOL INTRO – POSITIVE WORDS

Did you know that the words you choose tell the world quite a lot about you? Your words tell others what you are thinking, how you think, and if you are generally a positive or negative person.

POSITIVE WORDS have a powerful way of attracting POSITIVE ACTIONS, therefore getting in the habit of choosing more POSITIVE WORDS puts you in charge of how the world sees you and how you see yourself, which increases your POSITIVE ACTIONS automatically.

Negative words usually have the word "not" included in them. Words like "cannot," and "will not" or "could not" and "is not" are negative words. There are a bunch of other "not" words and they are negative words. Rather than picking a word with a "not" you can pick words that are POWERFUL, PRODUCTIVE, and POSITIVE.

HOW TO USE – POSITIVE WORDS

You can use POSITIVE WORDS by asking yourself the THREE P's. Are your words POWERFUL? Are they PRODUCTIVE? Are they POSITIVE? You can test to see if others are using POSITIVE WORDS by asking yourself if their words are POWERFUL, PRODUCTIVE, and POSITIVE.

Before you choose your words, test them out with the THREE P's. Are your words POWERFUL? PRODUCTIVE? POSITIVE?

MY GOGI TOOL POSITIVE ACTIONS

The weeks to study POSITIVE ACTIONS are:

2nd Week of February
2nd Week of May
2nd Week of August
2nd Week of November

KEYWORDS – POSITIVE ACTIONS

THE THREE P's
Is it POWERFUL?
Is it PRODUCTIVE?
Is it POSITIVE?

STATEMENT OF PURPOSE AND OWNERSHIP – POSITIVE ACTIONS

I know I have the power to transform my world through my POSITIVE ACTIONS. I choose my POSITIVE ACTIONS so I can move beyond my past and create my positive future.

OBJECTIVE – POSITIVE ACTIONS

Your goal this week is to be the boss of all your actions.

You will choose actions that are POWERFUL, PRODUCTIVE, and POSITIVE when you learn the tool POSITIVE ACTIONS.

TOOL INTRO – POSITIVE ACTIONS

Did you know that just doing one small POSITIVE ACTION may have a big positive result in your day? Yes, that is correct, even one small POSITIVE ACTION each day can help you a great deal in your ability to be the boss of your life.

POSITIVE ACTIONS are the small things you do, not necessarily the big things. The smaller POSITIVE ACTIONS are actually more powerful, because you can do more of them each day.

Did you know that if you have two to three POSITIVE ACTIONS picked out ahead of time, it is easier to overcome urges to make a poor decision?

HOW TO USE – POSITIVE ACTIONS

When you pick out two or three POSITIVE ACTIONS you will have them ready for your thought process. Having POSITIVE ACTIONS ready is important, because you may need to use them when the urge to make a poor choice seems to be pulling at you. Get your POSITIVE ACTIONS ready. Have them waiting.

Some examples of POSITIVE ACTIONS are: having a glass of water, walking around the block, exercising, picking up a good book, calling a sponsor or church friend, or cleaning up your living space.

GOGI Tool

MY GOGI TOOL CLAIM RESPONSIBILITY

The weeks to study CLAIM RESPONSIBILITY are:

3rd Week of February
3rd Week of May
3rd Week of August
3rd Week of November

KEYWORDS – CLAIM RESPONSIBILITY

AM I PROUD OF THIS CHOICE?
I am responsible for all my actions and all my reactions today.

STATEMENT OF PURPOSE AND OWNERSHIP – CLAIM RESPONSIBILITY

From this moment forward, I CLAIM RESPONSIBILITY for all my actions and all my reactions. All my actions and my reactions today are my responsibility and I CLAIM RESPONSIBILITY.

OBJECTIVE – CLAIM RESPONSIBILITY

This week you get to learn that the tool CLAIM RESPONSIBILITY puts you in charge of your reactions and actions today. CLAIM RESPONSIBILITY permits you to be the boss of how you handle problems and circumstances today.

TOOL INTRO – CLAIM RESPONSIBILITY

CLAIM RESPONSIBILITY allows you to focus on today. You do not need to focus on yesterday and you do not need to focus on tomorrow. With CLAIM RESPONSIBILITY you focus on today.

CLAIM RESPONSIBILITY lets you be the boss of your actions and of your reactions today. How you act today and how you react today is your decision. You are the boss.

HOW TO USE – CLAIM RESPONSIBILITY?

CLAIM RESPONSIBILITY is your power tool to help you control your actions and your reactions today. As a tool, CLAIM RESPONSIBILITY is not about the past, it is about your actions and reactions today.

You use CLAIM RESPONSIBILITY during the day when something happens or someone does something that would usually upset or concern you. With CLAIM RESPONSIBILITY you are being the boss of how you handle these situations.

Simply state: "Today I CLAIM RESPONSIBILITY for my actions and today I CLAIM RESPONSIBILITY for my reactions."

MY GOGI TOOL LET GO

The weeks to study LET GO are:

4th Week of February
4th Week of May
4th Week of August
4th Week of November

KEYWORDS – LET GO

HAND/SQUASH/TOSS.
When bothered, I put the feeling in my hand, squash it, and toss it away from me.

STATEMENT OF PURPOSE AND OWNERSHIP – LET GO

The best way to focus on living in the present and moving forward is if I LET GO of anything which has held me back. When I LET GO, I move forward and I set myself free.

OBJECTIVE – LET GO

Your goal this week is to practice the power of putting problems in your HAND, then SQUASHING them and TOSSING them away. This tool, called LET GO, will permit you to HAND/SQUASH/TOSS anything that might stand in your way of change.

TOOL INTRO – LET GO

GOGI knows there are things in your past that might seem too big to ever move beyond. Sometimes it seems as if the bad stuff has controlled and defined your life. That is sometimes a normal way to feel.

You can use the GOGI Tool called LET GO for the big things, but also for the daily little things. You can begin to use this tool to get past the daily irritations that happen to everyone.

HOW TO USE – LET GO

You use LET GO for the daily irritations, those things that seem to creep up on you and try to trip you up.

Someone bumps into you? Give it the HAND/SQUASH/TOSS and LET GO. Didn't get that job? Give it the LET GO. Didn't like how someone spoke to you? Give it the LET GO.
The more you use LET GO for the little daily things, the more powerfully it can help you with those old things that might still be bothering you.

GOGI Tool

MY GOGI TOOL FOR–GIVE

The weeks to study FOR–GIVE are:

1st Week of March
1st Week of June
1st Week of September
1st Week of December

KEYWORDS – FOR–GIVE

FOR ME TO GIVE, I NEED DISTANCE FROM HARM.
For me to give, I unhook from the past, and find my internal freedom.

STATEMENT OF PURPOSE AND OWNERSHIP – FOR–GIVE

FOR me to GIVE back to others I make sure I am safe from harm. FOR me to GIVE, I make sure I am safe.

OBJECTIVE – FOR–GIVE

This week you get to practice being the boss of how much past harm and past hurt you carry with you. You get to focus on being safe from more harm so that you can GIVE back to others and make your world a better place. FOR you to GIVE, you will learn to keep yourself safe.

TOOL INTRO – FOR–GIVE

For you to be really happy, you will eventually discover that you need to give your time and energy to others to help them. This is how lasting happiness is created. But FOR you to GIVE, you need to get yourself safe from harm. FOR you to be a GIVING individual, you must be getting distance from addiction or abuse. You must be SAFE ENOUGH TO GIVE.

FOR–GIVE as a GOGI TOOL requires that you get yourself in a safe enough position so you can begin to give back to others.

HOW TO USE – FOR–GIVE

As a tool, FOR–GIVE is about being safe enough for you to give back. This means if the harm is really close, you need to get to safety. If your addiction is the harm, you need to get to the safety offered by programs, churches, sober societies, and other support systems.

You need to be a sufficient distance from the person or circumstance that causes you harm. It is nearly impossible to forgive when the danger is right there in front of you. In fact, it is not wise to place an alcoholic in a bar, an addict next to a needle, or a thief next to unguarded jewels. FOR–GIVE is about protection. Make sure you and everyone around you is safe enough FOR you to GIVE back and FOR you to be the GIVING person you were meant to be.

MY GOGI TOOL WHAT IF

The weeks to study WHAT IF are:

2nd Week of March
2nd Week of June
2nd Week of September
2nd Week of December

KEYWORDS – WHAT IF

WHAT IF I AM NOT MY PAST?
No to the past = yes to the future.

STATEMENT OF PURPOSE AND OWNERSHIP – WHAT IF

WHAT IF permits me to see possibilities I might not otherwise realize. Today, I ask myself, WHAT IF I am not my past? WHAT IF I reached my goal? WHAT IF I actually improved my life today, tomorrow, and the next day?

OBJECTIVE – WHAT IF

Your goal this week is to be the boss of your future. You do this by asking the WHAT IF question, because when you look at the possible outcome for the future you will make better decisions in the present. WHAT IF is the tool you can use to build your positive future.

TOOL INTRO – WHAT IF

The tool WHAT IF is really cool because it gives you a glimpse into what might be possible. You can use WHAT IF for the negative to avoid negative outcomes. You can also use WHAT IF for the positive, to see new positive possibilities. WHAT IF is your ability to look into the future and see the likely outcome of any action you take. With this ability, you can set goals for yourself and clearly see the benefit of working toward a positive outcome. WHAT IF you are not your past? This critical question frees you to become a benefit to society because of your past! WHAT IF you are needed as the solution?

HOW TO USE – WHAT IF

You can use the GOGI Tool WHAT IF for everything you do during the day. WHAT IF you wake up early? WHAT IF you don't? WHAT IF you go to that meeting? WHAT IF you don't? WHAT IF places you in charge, because you are choosing every minute of the day what you want to endorse in your life. You are checking out the possible outcomes with the WHAT IF tool and you are clearly stating the direction of your life from now onward. WHAT IF can permit you a glimpse into the future. You can say "WHAT IF I don't go to a meeting and I start thinking about drinking?" And you can also say, "WHAT IF I do go to a meeting and I am able to sit with other people who are on a positive path?" WHAT IF gives you a snapshot of what is likely to happen with your decision.

GOGI Tool

MY GOGI TOOL REALITY CHECK

The weeks to study REALITY CHECK are:

3rd Week of March
3rd Week of June
3rd Week of September
3rd Week of December

KEYWORDS – REALITY CHECK

TEN AND TWO RULE
Ten steps forward and two steps back is still eight steps ahead.

STATEMENT OF PURPOSE AND OWNERSHIP – REALITY CHECK

I know I am going to make mistakes along the way, but REALITY CHECK lets me quickly correct my mistakes. Today, I agree to get right back on track with REALITY CHECK when I do something that is not perfect.

OBJECTIVE – REALITY CHECK

Your goal this week is to realize that you are human and you will make mistakes, but that does not mean you are not successful. This week's tool, REALITY CHECK, permits you to be the boss and recover from bad decisions quickly.

TOOL INTRO – REALITY CHECK

The fact is you are human. You are not perfect. You will make bad decisions. GOGI realizes and accepts that humans make poor decisions. However, GOGI realizes that humans do not need to remain in bad decision-making mode.

If you take ten steps forward and two steps backward, you are still eight steps ahead. With GOGI, REALITY CHECK states that we focus on the GOOD and the PROGRESS rather than the poor decisions.

For as long as you are human, you may make bad decisions, but your ability to get back on track quickly is your REALITY CHECK.

HOW TO USE – REALITY CHECK?

You can use REALITY CHECK with others and with yourself. Instead of focusing on the bad decisions, you focus on the improvements.

Focus on the positive. This will make it easier to overcome the disappointment that naturally comes when we make bad decisions.

Just say to yourself, "Ten steps forward and two steps back is still eight steps ahead." This will remind you that you are moving forward and give you your REALITY CHECK.

MY GOGI TOOL ULTIMATE FREEDOM

The weeks to study ULTIMATE FREEDOM are:

4th Week of March
4th Week of June
4th Week of September
4th Week of December

KEYWORDS – ULTIMATE FREEDOM

BEING FREE IS UP TO ME.
Living a life of service gives me ULTIMATE FREEDOM.

STATEMENT OF PURPOSE AND OWNERSHIP – ULTIMATE FREEDOM

I create ULTIMATE FREEDOM for myself when I live THE GOGI WAY. Through my service, I have ULTIMATE FREEDOM.

OBJECTIVE – ULTIMATE FREEDOM

Your goal this week is to practice creating freedom in your life by doing good things, even when no one is looking. ULTIMATE FREEDOM is this week's tool; and you can be the boss of your level of freedom when you practice ULTIMATE FREEDOM each day.

TOOL INTRO – ULTIMATE FREEDOM

ULTIMATE FREEDOM is a feeling inside you that no person and no situation can take away. ULTIMATE FREEDOM is also something you are in charge of creating for yourself. And, ULTIMATE FREEDOM is available for everyone, not just a few people who have something you do not.

ULTIMATE FREEDOM is the freedom that comes when you decide to live your life in service of others. When you choose to live your life for something more than your own desires and needs, you begin to feel the little sparks of ULTIMATE FREEDOM.

HOW TO USE – ULTIMATE FREEDOM

You can use the tool ULTIMATE FREEDOM at any time. All you need to do is focus your attention on being of service and helping to make a situation better.

You use ULTIMATE FREEDOM by moving into a POSITIVE ACTION that helps someone else. When you practice this way of living long enough, you may find yourself beginning to live in ULTIMATE FREEDOM every day, and your life will be truly, forever, ultimately happy.

KNOW YOUR GOGI
Positive Words.
Boss of My Brain.
Tools of The Body.
Positive Thoughts.
Choice.
Let Go.
Five Second Lightswitch.
Tools of
Tools of Moving Forward.
Claim Responsibility.
What If.
Tools of Creation.
Forgive.
Belly Breathing.
Positive Actions.
Ultimate Freedom.
Reality Check.
Dustin Jeffries '16
GOGI
www.gettingoutbygoingin.org

INCREASING MY PEACE – ACCOUNTABILITY BOX

DO YOU WANT CREDIT FOR THIS COURSE? REMEMBER TO KEEP TRACK OF YOUR DAILY STUDY BY COMPLETING THE INFORMATION BELOW TO GET YOUR CREDIT.

The month is_________________; The day is ________________; The year is________; Solo study or group? ______________

Week 1

INCREASING YOUR PEACE WITH BOSS OF MY BRAIN

To study the same tool as all other GOGI students, you may wish to study this chapter on:
1st week of January
1st week of April
1st week of July
1st week of October

PREPARING TO SUCCEED THIS WEEK

In this book or other GOGI materials, read the sections that mention the GOGI Tool BOSS OF MY BRAIN. Reading these sections of a GOGI book will give you great power to understand and apply this tool immediately in your life. You will also do better in your coursework when you read more about this tool in your other GOGI books.

What is the title of the GOGI book or books you have to study this week's tool? ____________________

____

On what pages did you find information about BOSS OF MY BRAIN? ____________________

____

What are the keywords for BOSS OF MY BRAIN? ____________________________

____

*What did you read that interested you?*____________________________________

____

*According to the GOGI Calendar, which weeks of the year do GOGI students study BOSS OF MY BRAIN?*____

____

____

What do you like, personally, about this tool? ____________________________

____

____

____

____

INCREASING MY PEACE – ACCOUNTABILITY BOX

DO YOU WANT CREDIT FOR THIS COURSE? REMEMBER TO KEEP TRACK OF YOUR DAILY STUDY BY COMPLETING THE INFORMATION BELOW TO GET YOUR CREDIT.

The month is________________; The day is ________________; The year is__________; Solo study or group? ____________

Have you read about this tool in this book yet? If not, you are cheating yourself of important information that will help you be the best version of you. Before you start with this week's study, please do yourself a favor and take a moment to read about this tool in this and other GOGI books. Then, continue with today's study.

Day 1 – KEEP YOUR POWER, don't give it away

BOSS OF MY BRAIN is a very powerful tool for anyone wishing to keep their power and not let others control their thoughts or actions. With this tool, you can make the final decision regarding how you act and how you react to others and the world around you. When you use BOSS OF MY BRAIN, it places you in control and you decide if anger is your best response, or if you want to choose a different response. BOSS OF MY BRAIN reminds you that no one makes your choices for you. No one is the boss of your decisions. No one forces you to lose your temper.

What do you think when you read that no one "forces" you to lose your temper? ________________

____

____

____

____

Many people say, "he made me so mad," or "I couldn't just let him do that, I had to do something." They oftentimes use the other person's choices and behaviors to dictate how they will respond. "She made me" and "It's her fault" are common statements used by people.

Have you said that someone "made" you angry or that it was someone's "fault" that you reacted out of anger? Who has "made" you angry? Whose "fault" is it when you lose your temper? __________

____

____

____

When you blame another person, you turn the control and power over to that person. You give the other person control over you when you point the finger at them. What do you think about the statement below, which was shared with GOGI by a prisoner serving a life sentence for killing someone out of anger over a girlfriend's choice to be with another man. He said, "When I blame her for my actions, I am giving her the power and control over me. When I know that my decisions and my anger are MY choice, then I am a better person and less likely to blow my top in the future."

What does this make you think about your own anger? ________________________

____

____

____

INCREASING MY PEACE – ACCOUNTABILITY BOX

DO YOU WANT CREDIT FOR THIS COURSE? REMEMBER TO KEEP TRACK OF YOUR DAILY STUDY BY COMPLETING THE INFORMATION BELOW TO GET YOUR CREDIT.

The month is__________________; The day is ________________; The year is_________; Solo study or group? ______________

LIFE HAPPENS

Let's say a guy named JJ calls his girlfriend and she does not accept the call. He calls a friend of hers and she says that the girlfriend has a new boyfriend, that she is pregnant, and she does not have the courage to tell him. JJ slams the phone receiver against the wall, it breaks, and he gets written up for destroying property. When meeting with the officer giving him the write-up, he can describe what he did in two ways:

Sentence #1 - "She made me so mad, I had no choice."

Sentence #2 - "I got so angry at what she did that I overreacted."

*Which statement permits JJ to keep his power and which statement allows the girlfriend to have power over JJ's actions? Why?*____

____

____

____

Let's say that JJ makes his decisions with the SMART PART of his brain. He goes back to his room, does 200 push-ups instead of breaking the phone.

What else might he do to remain in a POSITIVE DECISION-MAKING mode? ________________

____

____

What are other things he can do to KEEP HIS POWER and not let the girlfriend be his excuse for remaining angry? ____

____

____

____

If JJ were your cellie/roommate, what might you tell him? _____________________________

____

____

How might you remind him to use BOSS OF MY BRAIN? _______________________________

____

____

____

INCREASING MY PEACE – ACCOUNTABILITY BOX

DO YOU WANT CREDIT FOR THIS COURSE? REMEMBER TO KEEP TRACK OF YOUR DAILY STUDY BY COMPLETING THE INFORMATION BELOW TO GET YOUR CREDIT.

The month is__________________; The day is ________________; The year is__________; Solo study or group? __________

Day 2 – THE EMOTIONAL PART

As you have read in any of the GOGI books, you know with BOSS OF MY BRAIN you can choose to use the SMART PART when you make your decisions. You can also choose to use the EMOTIONAL PART of your brain as you choose how to respond or react. Or, you can choose to use the OLD HABIT PART thinking to direct your reactions. You are, ultimately, the boss of your choices when you use the tool BOSS OF MY BRAIN.

What does it mean to you to know that you are the boss and you can choose how you respond to things? That no person can "make" you get angry beyond your willingness to be angry? What does that mean to you? ____

____

____

This is pure fact: it is normal to have emotions about things that happen. It is also normal to have emotions about the actions of others. And, it is completely normal to dislike something, or to feel mad, bad, or sad. These feelings are normal. What is not to your advantage is to let these normal emotions explode into a series of actions and reactions you later regret.

What are some of the most common reasons you feel angry? Is it the actions of others that bother you most? Or your own actions? ____

____

*Does your anger sometimes lead to violence?*________________________________

Or is drug use or drinking your response to anger? __________________________

Do you run away from people or situations? ______________________________

Do you get angry at other people who had very little to do with the problem? ____________

____

*Do you retaliate and resort to violence to resolve the problem?*____________________

____

Do you withdraw from others or need time alone? ___________________________

____

People have many ways they deal with anger. What is your own personal response to things that make you angry? ____

____

Oftentimes, we respond to anger in a way that is similar to how we saw anger handled in our childhood. Who did you watch growing up that handled their anger in a manner that reminds you of how you now handle situations that anger you? Did you like how that person handled situations? Do you want to be like them? ______________________________

____

INCREASING MY PEACE – ACCOUNTABILITY BOX

DO YOU WANT CREDIT FOR THIS COURSE? REMEMBER TO KEEP TRACK OF YOUR DAILY STUDY BY COMPLETING THE INFORMATION BELOW TO GET YOUR CREDIT.

The month is________________; The day is ______________; The year is________; Solo study or group? ____________

LIFE HAPPENS

Let's say our friend JJ finds out that he is being transferred to a place he knows is impossible for his family to visit. They didn't visit anyway, but now he knows they will never visit. He is beyond angry and just wants to hit someone, or something. Hitting something has always helped to relieve the pressure he feels. He feels like he is going to explode. Unfortunately, it just so happens that a very disagreeable officer is on duty and the C.O. is pushing every button JJ has ever had. JJ gets even angrier when the officer cuts his shower short for some reason.

Of the reactions below, please circle which one is SMART PART THINKING, which is EMOTIONAL PART THINKING, and which is OLD HABIT PART THINKING.

OPTION ONE - JJ remembers that the guy in the room next to him got sent to Administrative Segregation last week for raising his fist and aggressively approaching this same officer. JJ is not interested in spending the next 30 days in Administrative Segregation trying to explain how this officer is provoking problems in the housing unit. Instead, he returns to his room and does 200 push-ups to relieve some of his anger and energy.

What part of his brain is the boss at that moment when he decides to return to his room and do push-ups?

Please circle one: *SMART PART* *EMOTIONAL PART* *OLD HABIT PART*

OPTION TWO - *JJ feels the anger boiling inside him and he feels no control over his anger. He feels as if things are getting out of control, that he is going to "lose it" and what will happen is not pretty.*

What form of thinking is the boss at this moment?

Please circle one: *SMART PART* *EMOTIONAL PART* *OLD HABIT PART*

OPTION THREE - JJ knows that his left hook is really solid and is his best shot at teaching this officer not to mess with him. He feels his fist getting tight and he is ready to rock and roll. His emotions are too intense for words, or rational decisions. What comes after he hits this officer doesn't really matter much to JJ.

What form of thinking is this?

Please circle one: *SMART PART* *EMOTIONAL PART* *OLD HABIT PART*

*In looking at your own reactions to things, would you say you most frequently let the SMART PART, the EMOTIONAL PART, or the OLD HABIT PART be in control of your life? Why?*______________

____

____

____

____

INCREASING MY PEACE – ACCOUNTABILITY BOX

DO YOU WANT CREDIT FOR THIS COURSE? REMEMBER TO KEEP TRACK OF YOUR DAILY STUDY BY COMPLETING THE INFORMATION BELOW TO GET YOUR CREDIT.

The month is________________; The day is ________________; The year is__________; Solo study or group? __________

Day 3 – THE OLD HABIT PART

Your brain is similar to a very powerful computer. When you do, or think the same thing, over and over for 21-28 days, your brain thinks that you want this to be a new habit, and your brain begins to create a pattern of brain activity so that your new habit can be developed.

Once your new habit is in place, it gets tucked away towards the back of your brain and becomes "automatic" and you don't really need to think about it any more, it just happens. When you repeat something for years and years, this habit becomes strongly reinforced, and it is oftentimes a big challenge to stop this habit from automatically kicking into full gear.

Were you aware that your brain is like a powerful computer? Does it make sense that things you repeat over and over become habits? What does that make you think about the habits you have developed?

____

____

____

____

At GOGI, we call the automatic things we do OLD HABIT PART THINKING. You are in your OLD HABIT PART THINKING when you rely on, or permit, the automatic part of your brain to run the show and be the boss. In some cases, this is a good thing, like the habit of drinking water or exercising which may become automatic for you. In other cases, like smoking cigarettes, drinking or using drugs, cussing, or resorting to anger and violence, an automatic habit is not in your best interest. In cases like these, letting the OLD HABIT PART be the boss is a big problem.

What are some of the habits you have that you think the OLD HABIT PART of your brain runs automatically? ____

____

____

____

The OLD HABIT PART of your brain is located at the back of your head, right above your neck. This is where automatic stuff gets stored. If you put your hand at the back of your head above your neck, this is where all your old habits get stored.

What are some of the old habits that you are willing to swap out for new and improved versions of things you want in your life? What are some new habits that might support your self-improvement?

____

____

INCREASING MY PEACE – ACCOUNTABILITY BOX

DO YOU WANT CREDIT FOR THIS COURSE? REMEMBER TO KEEP TRACK OF YOUR DAILY STUDY BY COMPLETING THE INFORMATION BELOW TO GET YOUR CREDIT.

The month is_______________; The day is _______________; The year is_________; Solo study or group? _______________

LIFE HAPPENS

Let's visit our friend JJ once again. JJ is having a really good day, considering his eight-foot cell and two-inch mattress circumstance. He reads his GOGI book and suddenly realizes that he always hated how angry and violent his mother would get, but he realizes that he handles situations just like his mom. This angers him even more and he blames HER for not being different. And, he also blames the father he never knew for not being there.

Then, he gets even ANGRIER because the GOGI book states that his anger is his CHOICE. He totally disagrees with GOGI and is ready to toss his GOGI book in the trash, but he needs a certificate to show the Board that he is a changed man. He doesn't toss the book, but he can't believe that his anger is a choice he makes.

Let's say you get moved into JJ's room and he rants on and on about GOGI not understanding him, his mother being to blame, and how much he hates his father who was never there. What do you tell JJ? _

____

____

JJ listens to you. You seem to speak in a way that gets him to understand that GOGI isn't accusing him of causing all the problems, but that he is actually able to rise above any situation and use the SMART PART of his brain to decide how to respond. You ask him to consider his OLD HABIT PART THINKING. He turns the tables on you and asks YOU to tell him about YOUR challenges in creating new habits and the power of OLD HABIT PART THINKING.

What do you share with him about yourself and why? _______________________

____

____

As you and JJ talk, long past lights out, you realize that you have some old habits that really need to be rethought. Maybe now is the time to LET GO of some anger and resentments that have held you back. You know you have changes you need to make in your automatic thinking. You close your eyes, making a mental list of these things, and in the morning you write them down so you don't forget.

What are the things you write down that you want to switch up and make not so automatic? ______

____

How did talking with JJ help you realize your own journey of self-improvement? Many GOGI students find that sharing experiences and sharing their tools helps them become better friends and advocates for positive thinking. What do you think about this opinion? _______________

____

____

INCREASING MY PEACE – ACCOUNTABILITY BOX

DO YOU WANT CREDIT FOR THIS COURSE? REMEMBER TO KEEP TRACK OF YOUR DAILY STUDY BY COMPLETING THE INFORMATION BELOW TO GET YOUR CREDIT.

The month is________________; The day is ______________; The year is________; Solo study or group? ____________

Day 4 – THE SMART PART

The SMART PART of your brain is located right behind your forehead. Sometimes people will say, "Think!" and they will touch their foreheads at the same time. This is because the smart thinking that you do is happening right behind your forehead. Technically speaking, it is the area where "executive functioning" happens, but keeping it simple, at GOGI we just call it SMART PART THINKING.

When you experience something new, like moving to a new location, laying down in a different bed for the first time, going to a sink for the first time, or going to chow for the first time, your brain is using the SMART PART to assess everything that is happening, and everything you are seeing. Things that are new and different get processed at the front part of your brain because you are going to need to decide what you think and how to react or respond to the new information.

In the past year, what new things has your brain had to process? What new experiences have come your way in the past year? ____

____

____

As you experience new things, your brain filters things through the SMART PART to permit you to assess if something is good or bad, if you like it or you don't like it. You actually form an emotional "opinion" about things, assessing judgments on things like, "I don't like this room," or "this bed is too hard," or "metal sinks are easy to clean," or "the chow hall is way too noisy." You assign assessments, which require that you use the middle of your brain, a place GOGI calls the EMOTIONAL PART. This is where you assign good or bad, like or dislike, safety or danger.

In the past year, what new things has your SMART PART processed that you then created an opinion or belief about? What are some of the new experiences you've had and how do you feel about them?

____

____

Once you grow accustomed to a routine, the information no longer needs to be filtered through your SMART PART. It gets stored as a "habit" in the back of your brain. You can still have an "opinion" about it, you can still feel an "emotion" because of it, but it becomes a habit.

In the past year, can you think of things that might have become automatic for you? Things that were new to you not long ago, but things that are now familiar and "regular" to your daily routine?

____

How do you think you might be able to continue to use your SMART PART when you are faced with challenges and you get upset and angry? Knowing what you know about the SMART PART of your brain, how might this help you? ________________________________

____

____

INCREASING MY PEACE – ACCOUNTABILITY BOX

DO YOU WANT CREDIT FOR THIS COURSE? REMEMBER TO KEEP TRACK OF YOUR DAILY STUDY BY COMPLETING THE INFORMATION BELOW TO GET YOUR CREDIT.

The month is________________; The day is ________________; The year is________; Solo study or group? ____________

LIFE HAPPENS

JJ is doing much better now that you are in the room with him. He is reading his GOGI book and not wanting to toss it against the wall every other sentence. In fact, he was reading and asked if he could ask you a few questions. He wants to know if the SMART PART of his brain could have been damaged by all the drugs, anger, and fighting, or if, maybe, his SMART PART is just not as developed as everyone else and he is doomed to make bad decisions.

Based on what you have read in your GOGI book, what can you tell JJ about the tool BOSS OF MY BRAIN and if it will work for him? ____

____

Refer to your GOGI book, if needed, and quote something or write down a page number for JJ to read. ____

____

____

JJ asks you if you were always calm and cool headed. You smile. You know you were once like JJ but you have grown, learned, and practiced your GOGI Tools. You are a very different person now, and you feel a sense of accomplishment that he would consider you calm and cool.

Share with JJ what your journey was like, how you learned to respond and react to life's challenges in a more mature and powerful way using your GOGI Tools, or how your journey is continuing to this day, and how you are applying tools to your life. ______________________________

JJ, there was a time when... ____

____

At some point I realized... ____

____

____

For me, change was... ____

____

____

I can handle things better now because... ______________________________

____

My hope for you is that... ____

____

INCREASING MY PEACE – ACCOUNTABILITY BOX

DO YOU WANT CREDIT FOR THIS COURSE? REMEMBER TO KEEP TRACK OF YOUR DAILY STUDY BY COMPLETING THE INFORMATION BELOW TO GET YOUR CREDIT.

The month is______________; The day is ______________; The year is________; Solo study or group? __________

Day 5 – WHICH ONE IS IN CHARGE?

In every decision you choose, there is always one part of your brain that is more in charge than the others. You can be using all three parts, the SMART PART, the EMOTIONAL PART, and the OLD HABIT PART all at the same time, but there will be one boss, one part that is more in control than the others.

INCREASING YOUR PEACE may be as simple as asking yourself which part of your brain is the boss? When you acknowledge what part of your brain is the boss, you are choosing your reaction, regardless of what that reaction may be.

How can you make it very easy to remember to ask yourself, "Which part of my brain is in charge?" Is there something you can do, or some way you can remind yourself that you and only you can use BOSS OF MY BRAIN in your decision-making? ____________________________

____

____

Understanding that you can direct your brain to use different areas in your decision-making process can be a very new concept for many people. The idea that if you are emotional you can redirect your thoughts to the SMART PART of your brain is oftentimes a new concept. The idea that you can create new and positive habits to replace processes in your OLD HABIT PART is a concept that might be confusing.

What do you think about this concept that you can choose what part of your brain is the boss? _____

____

____

What do you think about filling up the OLD HABIT PART of your brain with positive habits instead of the worn-out bad habits that never really worked for you anyway? ____________________

____

____

One GOGI student stated that even though he would be spending the rest of his life in prison, it was nice to know that he was the boss of his own brain and no one could take that job from him. He stated that he could be a good boss, or a bad boss, but he was always going to be the boss of his brain.

*Do you agree with his assessment of ownership of his own brain? Do you think that his life in prison will be happier and more positive as a result of this perspective and understanding? Why or why not?*____

____

____

INCREASING MY PEACE – ACCOUNTABILITY BOX

DO YOU WANT CREDIT FOR THIS COURSE? REMEMBER TO KEEP TRACK OF YOUR DAILY STUDY BY COMPLETING THE INFORMATION BELOW TO GET YOUR CREDIT.

The month is________________; The day is ______________; The year is________; Solo study or group? ____________

LIFE HAPPENS

Poor JJ. He just can't seem to break free from his old perspective. He was doing fine for a few days and then he gets a letter. His girlfriend wrote him a letter stating that she needed "time to think." Obviously, he tells you, she has not talked to her friend and does not realize he already knows she is pregnant and hooked up with (what he calls) "some loser" who doesn't have a job, car, and still lives with his mother. "She makes me so mad," he says.

What do you say in response to this statement that SHE MAKES him mad? ____________________

You now know that to change an old habit and fill the OLD HABIT PART with new options, it is important to create new and more positive habits. You consider the fact that you, too, need a few new habits. You propose to JJ that the two of you start a workout routine to do each and every day, as a new habit. JJ agrees that sitting around wanting to punch the block wall is not exactly getting him anywhere so he joins you.

How do you describe the process of building a new habit that can be stored in the back of your brain in the OLD HABIT PART? How can you describe to him the process of replacing the old habits with new and positive ones? ____________________

It turns out that JJ is quite consistent and demanding when it comes to this new habit of working out every day. He seems to be taking this new habit thing a bit too seriously and wakes you up in the middle of the night with his leg lifts, squats, and 200 arm curls with his stack of books. You are thrilled that he no longer talks about his girlfriend, but he is annoying you with his obsession to turn his stomach into a six-pack of pure muscle.

You appreciate JJ's enthusiasm, but you are getting a little angry and wonder if he is playing some sort of trick on you in order to get you rattled. You are not sure you can take one more night of midnight squats and you are ready to start yelling at him when you think twice. How do you process this irritation and how can you get a positive result out of a negative situation?

INCREASING MY PEACE – ACCOUNTABILITY BOX

DO YOU WANT CREDIT FOR THIS COURSE? REMEMBER TO KEEP TRACK OF YOUR DAILY STUDY BY COMPLETING THE INFORMATION BELOW TO GET YOUR CREDIT.

The month is________________; The day is ______________; The year is________; Solo study or group? __________

Day 6 – YOU ARE ALWAYS THE BOSS

Do you think your life would have been a little different if you were taught by your family and at school to use the tool BOSS OF MY BRAIN? If, as a child, you were taught that you had three parts of your brain that mattered, the SMART PART, the EMOTIONAL PART, and the OLD HABIT PART, do you think you would have made different decisions?

What are some of the decisions you've made in the past that would've been different if you were using BOSS OF MY BRAIN? ____

____

____

____

____

As humans, our brain continues to learn, mold, and shape in the direction we tell our brains to focus. We continue to learn and mold our brain until we die, even if we think we are not smart or damaged or that we have taken so many drugs that our brain is no longer functioning well. The truth is, if we want our brain to learn about cars, we simply need to read and watch information about cars. If we want to have our brain be busy with drugs, we need to be around, use, think, and talk about drugs. If we want our brain to be a good student at school, we simply need to expose our brain to study assignments. Our brains will be good at whatever we direct our brains to do.

If you are the best boss of your brain, what would you want your brain to learn? Would this help you "manage" your anger? Some GOGI students say that learning something new pushes out the old anger and they can LET GO of feelings from the past. Would learning something new and positive help replace the emotions of anger a little? How might it help? ______________________

____

____

____

When you understand that you, and only you, are the boss of your thoughts and actions, then you can make decisions that benefit you. You do not need to fall victim and permit the actions of others to dictate who you are and what you do. When you are the boss, you do not need to blame others. It is YOU who is in charge of your life.

In understanding that you are the boss of every thought and every reaction you choose, does that change how you feel about anger? Does it empower you to consider your anger in a new way?

____

____

____

INCREASING MY PEACE – ACCOUNTABILITY BOX

DO YOU WANT CREDIT FOR THIS COURSE? REMEMBER TO KEEP TRACK OF YOUR DAILY STUDY BY COMPLETING THE INFORMATION BELOW TO GET YOUR CREDIT.

The month is________________; The day is ______________; The year is________; Solo study or group? ___________

LIFE HAPPENS

You and JJ are spreading your "GOGI workout routine" to others in your housing unit. You do push-ups to the keywords of BOSS OF MY BRAIN and you recite the statement of purpose and ownership, the objectives, and even review the calendar dates during your GOGI workout. On the yard, you have quite the workout crew, with five or six different guys joining to work out with you two.

JJ has decided that if he ever gets released from custody, that he wants to be a fitness instructor with a cause, the kind of guy who works with troubled youth and teaches them about their body while teaching them the GOGI Tools. Thankfully, he is not working out in the middle of the night, and all is well. You get called into the counselor's office to be told that you are being transferred to a prison you know has a bad reputation for no programming and heavy politics. You must break the news to JJ.

What do you tell JJ about your transfer, about breaking up the wonderful workout program you two have created, and about using your GOGI Tools? What will you share with him? ___________

____

____

____

On the last day of your stay at this prison, JJ gathers your workout crew together and each man states what he appreciates about what you brought to their lives. JJ is beaming and he has truly found his calling in life. You are touched that teaching them BOSS OF MY BRAIN has dramatically influenced how they each deal with anger and frustration. You catch yourself fighting back a single tear that wants to make its way down your cheek. You are surprised. You aren't the crying type, but this kind of support is just too much.

The men ask you for words of wisdom as they each agree to continue to practice BOSS OF MY BRAIN. What do you tell your men? ___________________________________

____

____

On the bus ride to the new prison you have time to think. You consider who you were when you were once a slave to your anger and frustration. Now, men on the yard are telling you how grateful they are for your peaceful way of living. You know you have learned a lot and you are grateful for BOSS OF MY BRAIN because it permits you to help others in a simple and easy to understand manner. As the bus pulls up to the new institution, you consider what is ahead.

How important is it for you to use the SMART PART of your brain, even though you have been told that this prison is a lousy place to be? What can you do to remain positive, when all the odds are stacked up against you? ______________________________________

____

____

INCREASING MY PEACE – ACCOUNTABILITY BOX

DO YOU WANT CREDIT FOR THIS COURSE? REMEMBER TO KEEP TRACK OF YOUR DAILY STUDY BY COMPLETING THE INFORMATION BELOW TO GET YOUR CREDIT.

The month is_______________; The day is _______________; The year is________; Solo study or group? __________

Day 7 - Recap and Review

Write the STATEMENT OF PURPOSE AND OWNERSHIP for BOSS OF MY BRAIN. __________

What are the keywords for BOSS OF MY BRAIN? __________

What do you like about BOSS OF MY BRAIN? __________

How might BOSS OF MY BRAIN help you in making the most positive decisions? __________

What does HOLD ON TO YOUR POWER mean to you? __________

What does SMART PART mean to you? __________

What does EMOTIONAL PART mean to you? __________

What does OLD HABIT PART mean to you? __________

What does "who is in charge?" mean to you? __________

What does "you are the boss" mean to you? __________

This is art is a gift to GOGI from Keith E.

INCREASING MY PEACE – ACCOUNTABILITY BOX

DO YOU WANT CREDIT FOR THIS COURSE? REMEMBER TO KEEP TRACK OF YOUR DAILY STUDY BY COMPLETING THE INFORMATION BELOW TO GET YOUR CREDIT.

The month is________________; The day is ______________; The year is________; Solo study or group? ____________

YOUR PEACE PAGE

This page is provided for you to answer questions you may eventually be asked about your anger and your ability to choose another response.

Humans usually choose anger, rage, and violence when they are not aware of more positive options. Sometimes it feels as if there is no other option. Sometimes there is no other option. As you think about the times in your life when you got angry and this resulted in actions that you may now regret, please write about your choices at that time. Did you not know you had a choice? Was a peaceful choice too difficult? Was a peaceful choice impossible?

Use this page to review one critical time in your life, one particularly hostile relationship, or one situation when your choice could have been different, one where you were not the BOSS OF YOUR BRAIN. Why did you make the choice you made?

I remember a time when... ____

____

____

I was angry because... ____

____

____

I let my anger... ____

____

____

I now know that anger is... ____

____

____

____

I am learning BOSS OF MY BRAIN which helps me... ______________________________

____

____

If in a similar situation now, I would... ______________________________________

____

____

INCREASING MY PEACE – ACCOUNTABILITY BOX

DO YOU WANT CREDIT FOR THIS COURSE? REMEMBER TO KEEP TRACK OF YOUR DAILY STUDY BY COMPLETING THE INFORMATION BELOW TO GET YOUR CREDIT.

The month is__________________; The day is ______________; The year is________; Solo study or group? ____________

YOUR STRATEGY PAGE

This page is provided for you to answer questions you may eventually be asked about strategies you have for your future. Start to formalize a plan so that when life serves up its inevitable challenges, you are prepared to handle them by INCREASING YOUR PEACE.

Humans are always more successful when they practice and plan how to handle things. When humans are unprepared or have not practiced or planned, they are often less successful than those who DO practice and plan. This is your page to write down a particular scenario you believe you may face in the future. Write this scenario down and then write about your plan to overcome all obstacles using your tools and your thoughtful planning.

This strategy could be related to a job, a relationship, a C.O., a move, a release, a denial of release, a death in the family, or even a smelly cellie. You build your plan on exactly how you can INCREASE THE PEACE in that situation.

*The situation is...*____

____

The challenge I face is... ____

____

*The temptation is to...*____

____

I have another choice now. I can... ____

____

*Tell us what you have learned so far in this course that will help you in your efforts to be a better person? How might this course help you make better decisions?*______________________

____

____

I have learned... ____

____

____

____

____

____

____

INCREASING MY PEACE – ACCOUNTABILITY BOX

DO YOU WANT CREDIT FOR THIS COURSE? REMEMBER TO KEEP TRACK OF YOUR DAILY STUDY BY COMPLETING THE INFORMATION BELOW TO GET YOUR CREDIT.

The month is________________; The day is ______________; The year is________; Solo study or group? ____________

DEEP DIVING - Getting to the bottom of it

Here are two pages for you. On these pages, we want to know about your journey with your own anger. We want to know what caused your anger and how you are working towards increasing your peace. Refer to what you have studied this week and know that each week you will be permitted to jot down your thoughts and experiences related to your past, your present, and your future.

*Growing up, anger seemed to be...*____

____

____

*I first realized I was angry when I...*____

____

____

*The anger I experienced in my youth was...*____

____

____

____

*In my family, anger was...*____

____

____

*As I continue to grow and learn, I realize that anger was...*____

____

____

____

*I would like to develop the power within my mind to...*____

____

____

*I will know I have increased my level of peace when I...*____

____

____

DO YOU WANT CREDIT FOR THIS COURSE? REMEMBER TO KEEP TRACK OF YOUR DAILY STUDY BY COMPLETING THE INFORMATION BELOW TO GET YOUR CREDIT.

The month is__________________; The day is ________________; The year is_________; Solo study or group? ______________

DEEP DIVING

Use these pages to write down how you might describe your own rehabilitation, or how to explain to a loved one how you are no longer the person you once were. However you use these pages, let them reflect your insight, your understanding, and your ability to be the best person you can be - today!

*This is what I hope for my future...*____

Here is one example of how I have improved in my ability to choose something other than anger...

I am learning and growing every day. Most recently I learned that I... ______________

*The most wonderful thing that could happen is if...*_______________________________

This art is a gift to GOGI from Nicholas M.

DO YOU WANT CREDIT FOR THIS COURSE? REMEMBER TO KEEP TRACK OF YOUR DAILY STUDY BY COMPLETING THE INFORMATION BELOW TO GET YOUR CREDIT.

The month is________________; The day is ________________; The year is________; Solo study or group? ____________

Week 2

INCREASING YOUR PEACE WITH BELLY BREATHING

To study the same tool as all other GOGI students, you may wish to study this chapter on:
2nd Week of January
2nd Week of April
2nd Week of July
2nd Week of October

PREPARING TO SUCCEED THIS WEEK

In this book or other GOGI materials, read those sections that mention BELLY BREATHING. Reading these sections of the book will give you great power to understand and apply this tool immediately in your life. You will also do better in your coursework when you read more about the tool in your GOGI books.

What is the title of the GOGI book or books you have to study this week's tool? __________________

____

On what pages did you find information about BELLY BREATHING? __________________________

____

*What are the keywords for BELLY BREATHING?*____

____

*What did you read that interested you?*____

____

*According to the GOGI Calendar, which weeks of the year do most GOGI students study BELLY BREATHING?*____

____

____

What do you like, personally, about this tool? ____________________________________

____

____

____

____

INCREASING MY PEACE – ACCOUNTABILITY BOX

DO YOU WANT CREDIT FOR THIS COURSE? REMEMBER TO KEEP TRACK OF YOUR DAILY STUDY BY COMPLETING THE INFORMATION BELOW TO GET YOUR CREDIT.

The month is__________________; The day is ________________; The year is________; Solo study or group? ______________

Have you read about these tools in this book yet? If not, you are cheating yourself of important information that will help you be the best version of you. Before you start with this week's study, please do yourself a favor and take a moment to read about these tools in this and other GOGI books. Then, continue with today's study.

Day 1 – PEACE, it's in your belly

One GOGI student said that he found peace in his belly. When asked what he meant by that, he stated that once he learned how to breathe with air getting all the way down into his belly area like he was taught with the GOGI Tool called BELLY BREATHING, he did not get so angry and he found more peace of mind.

*What do you think when you read that a prisoner found more peace in his mind when he started to use BELLY BREATHING?*____

____

____

Based on what you have read so far in this course, do you think that BELLY BREATHING might help you to create more peace in your mind? Why? ________________________________

____

____

____

Please put one hand on your belly area and one hand on your chest area. Just leave them there for a few moments. Do you notice anything? Do you notice your chest moving or your belly moving every time you breathe in air? Did you know that when you are relaxed it is more likely that your belly will move as you breathe? Did you know that when you are stressed or angry, your body will breathe with your chest moving up and down more?

To use BELLY BREATHING, it is as simple as putting one hand on your chest and one on your belly area and seeing which one is moving. Of course, it is in your best interest to have your belly area doing all the breathing.

Write what you think about BELLY BREATHING and if you believe you will be able to use this tool every day to measure your level of frustration or relaxation. __________________________

____

____

____

____

____

DO YOU WANT CREDIT FOR THIS COURSE? REMEMBER TO KEEP TRACK OF YOUR DAILY STUDY BY COMPLETING THE INFORMATION BELOW TO GET YOUR CREDIT.

The month is________________; The day is ______________; The year is________; Solo study or group? ____________

LIFE HAPPENS

Maria never thought she would end up in prison, but there she sits, doing 85 percent of seven years for credit card fraud. Her mother took her three kids back to Mexico. Her husband took her girlfriend to fill the empty place in his bed. And now her bunkie is stressing because her phone card is missing and Maria seems to be the logical one to blame. After all, no one needs to make a phone call more than Maria right now.

Maria attended the GOGI INCREASING YOUR PEACE group meeting last night and they were reviewing BELLY BREATHING as the tool of the week. She learned that when she is using her BELLY BREATHING tool she makes smarter decisions. Her bunkie comes back from chow really heated up.

Bunkie: "Maria, you are going to pay me back - or give me back that phone card you stole from me, you @!%*%^&!!!"

To think clearly, Maria needs to use every tool she is learning. In the past, she just tried to lie to get out of trouble, but that does not seem to work these days. She just gets beat up because of her lies.

In your opinion, what GOGI Tool can Maria use, and how might she use this tool to handle this situation? What might she say to the bunkie who is coming at her ready for a fight? ____________

____

____

____

____

____

____

If Maria really wants to change her life, what advice would you give her? She seems to be at the bottom of the very bottom and has lost everything. What would you say to Maria? ____________

____

____

____

____

____

____

____

INCREASING MY PEACE – ACCOUNTABILITY BOX

DO YOU WANT CREDIT FOR THIS COURSE? REMEMBER TO KEEP TRACK OF YOUR DAILY STUDY BY COMPLETING THE INFORMATION BELOW TO GET YOUR CREDIT.

The month is________________; The day is ________________; The year is__________; Solo study or group? ____________

Day 2 – STRESS CAN BE YOUR FRIEND

At GOGI we know life is stressful and nothing is more stressful than living in a prison, a jail, or any other environment where anger, violence, and aggression are the norm. When people are stressed, they oftentimes get angry. Anger leads to violence. But, did you know that with using your GOGI Tools, you may focus all your energy toward increasing your own levels of peace of mind instead of getting stressed, angry, or violent? You can increase your peace using your GOGI Tools. Here is how.

The next time you hear or see someone who is stressed out or angry, turn your focus on your own breathing. If you can, put one hand on your belly and one hand on your chest to make sure air is getting to your belly area. Just try this today. Try it several times. When you hear an officer yell, someone in the next room having a fit, or when your mind starts racing toward things that get you angry, just put one hand on your belly and one on your chest.

*How many times did you turn your focus to BELLY BREATHING today when things around you were less than peaceful? What was happening around you that turned your focus to your own breathing? Was it an officer? Someone in a cell nearby?*________________________

____

____

*Did you know that athletes and performers often do better when they have a little bit of stress in their life? What do you think about the idea that stress can help you be uncomfortable enough that you to try something different or difficult so you can get rid of the stress?*____________________

____

____

Somehow, athletes and performers are able to turn their stress into a sincere desire to be their very best. If this approach works for athletes and performers, how might you use BELLY BREATHING when you experience stress and anger so that you, too, can focus on being your very best? ______

____

____

____

What might be your plan to turn a stressful situation into your focus on being the best person you can be? What might be your strategy for using your GOGI Tools to better handle stress and anger?

____

____

____

____

INCREASING MY PEACE – ACCOUNTABILITY BOX

DO YOU WANT CREDIT FOR THIS COURSE? REMEMBER TO KEEP TRACK OF YOUR DAILY STUDY BY COMPLETING THE INFORMATION BELOW TO GET YOUR CREDIT.

The month is_______________; The day is _______________; The year is________; Solo study or group? _____________

LIFE HAPPENS

Let's revisit our friend, Maria. For some reason, it seems all her ways of handling things just are not working too well for her. Her bunkie beat her up, tossed everything in her room, found the stolen calling card, and now Maria and her bunkie are sitting in AdSeg waiting to be interviewed. Maria sits on the two-inch mattress and wonders if things can get much worse. Just then, the floor Sergeant approaches her room and asks if she would be interested in reading a GOGI book.

"*@%^& NO!" Maria replies.

The Sergeant walks away and mumbles, "suit yourself." Maria breaks down into tears and her breathing becomes very short and stressed. She hits the door, and hurts her hand. She starts to cry even more. She knew that lying to her bunkie was not going to get her out of her situation.

Let's pretend you are able to patch into Maria's AdSeg room on a small TV screen on the brick wall and she is willing to listen to you. What would you say to Maria about her stress, anger, and violence? How could you get her to start using her tools to create more internal peace?

____

____

____

____

____

Complete this paragraph.

Maria, hey, It's me. I am studying GOGI and I am learning a few things. Let me share with you some thoughts about your situation. Let me recap what I know about some GOGI Tools and how you can use them. BELLY BREATHING... ____

____

Here is what I know based on my experience... ____

____

____

*My suggestion is that you...*____

____

____

____

____

INCREASING MY PEACE – ACCOUNTABILITY BOX

DO YOU WANT CREDIT FOR THIS COURSE? REMEMBER TO KEEP TRACK OF YOUR DAILY STUDY BY COMPLETING THE INFORMATION BELOW TO GET YOUR CREDIT.

The month is________________; The day is ______________; The year is________; Solo study or group? ____________

Day 3 – WHAT IS LOSS AVERSION?

It's a set of big words but simply defined the words LOSS AVERSION mean that as humans we are often willing to be miserable if we are not sure about the options and not sure things can get better. Crazy as it may sound, humans are wired so that we will choose to remain violent, angry, or stressed if we are unsure what being peaceful would create in our world. This is why at GOGI we don't want you to make huge and fast changes. That causes its own kind of stress and you don't need more stress added to your existing stress. That will only make you angrier. Rather than BIG and fast changes, we just want you to make TINY changes, little changes each day. Small changes each day let you grow more comfortable with your changes as you see them working in your life.

Today, practice BELLY BREATHING at least five different times during the day. This can be done before you get out of bed, or before you go to sleep. It can be done in the shower, as you dress, as you make your bunk, grab your books, sit down to eat, or before or during a conversation. BELLY BREATHING can be done anywhere.

What were, or will be, the five or more times you practiced BELLY BREATHING today? When you read about "loss aversion" how do you think practicing BELLY BREATHING for five times each day might help you become more comfortable with acting and reacting differently? ______________

____

____

____

Thinking about your life, how much of your anger or violence in the past do you think was simply a habit? How much of your past do you think might have been driven by "loss aversion" and not trusting or realizing there were any other possible ways for you to handle irritating situations?

____

____

____

____

____

Think of one time when you reacted in anger and violence. As you think about that one particular instance, do you think you were BELLY BREATHING? Were you even paying attention to your breathing? ____

____

____

____

INCREASING MY PEACE – ACCOUNTABILITY BOX

DO YOU WANT CREDIT FOR THIS COURSE? REMEMBER TO KEEP TRACK OF YOUR DAILY STUDY BY COMPLETING THE INFORMATION BELOW TO GET YOUR CREDIT.

The month is________________; The day is ______________; The year is________; Solo study or group? ____________

LIFE HAPPENS

Maria is moved from AdSeg onto another yard, a yard with a bunch of troublemakers and quite a bit of politics among the women. She has decided that she finally wants to do things differently, but how?

She starts to attend church services offered by a really nice Chaplain every Saturday. She starts signing up for workshops and classes as soon as the signup sheet is posted in the dayroom. Even though alcohol is not her thing, she starts to attend the AA meetings and realizes she might have an addiction to money and approval. She finds herself talking less and listening more. But, oddly enough, she is OK with this.

The one workshop she WILL NOT sign up for is the GOGI Workshop!

Knowing what you know about "loss aversion" what advice might you give to Maria when the signup sheet for GOGI gets posted and she is standing there with her three-inch pencil in her hand?

____

____

____

What might keep Maria from signing up? ______________________

____

____

____

____

*Why do you think Maria is so resistant to change? What possible "comfort" do you think she finds in doing the same thing over and over again? Do you think her stress, anger, and violence helps her cope, in a strange way? Can you relate at all to how Maria thinks?*______________

____

____

____

Do you know someone like Maria? Who? Why do you think they resist the positive? __________

____

____

____

____

INCREASING MY PEACE – ACCOUNTABILITY BOX

DO YOU WANT CREDIT FOR THIS COURSE? REMEMBER TO KEEP TRACK OF YOUR DAILY STUDY BY COMPLETING THE INFORMATION BELOW TO GET YOUR CREDIT.

The month is________________; The day is ______________; The year is________; Solo study or group? ____________

Day 4 – FILLING YOUR FEET

As GOGI grew across the nation, the prisoners who created the tools were invited to comment and help refine the tools so they were as effective as possible. BELLY BREATHING seemed to be a simple tool that did not need much explanation, but that was not the case.

One GOGI student, a prisoner, commented that no matter how hard he tried, the air simply did not get into his belly area. His chest would move up and down, but he believed his belly area simply didn't have the ability.

When you place one hand on your belly and one hand on your chest, does your belly expand and contract with every breath?

When we are angry or fearful, our breathing gets shallow and it is difficult to get the air into our entire body. If we are angry or fearful for a long period of time it seems like our body "forgets" how to breathe correctly.

When you get angry or fearful do you understand that your breathing probably changes and not enough oxygen is available to help you make positive decisions? ______________________________

____

____

When this GOGI student stated that it was impossible for his belly to move during his breathing, it was suggested that he forget about his belly for a moment and he sit still for a few seconds and imagine that his job was to breathe in such a way that his feet would fill up with air.

"Fill my feet?" he asked.

"Yep, see if when you breathe you can imagine getting air all the way to your toes," was the reply.

Today, sit still for a moment and try this little trick to get air into every bit of your body. See if you can imagine getting air all the way into your toes. What is it like to imagine getting air into your feet? Was it an odd feeling? Were you successful? ______________________________

____

____

____

Do you think this technique might work for someone who just can't seem to master BELLY BREATHING? ____

____

____

____

INCREASING MY PEACE – ACCOUNTABILITY BOX

DO YOU WANT CREDIT FOR THIS COURSE? REMEMBER TO KEEP TRACK OF YOUR DAILY STUDY BY COMPLETING THE INFORMATION BELOW TO GET YOUR CREDIT.

The month is________________; The day is ______________; The year is________; Solo study or group? __________

LIFE HAPPENS

It just so happens that the prison where Maria lives announced that they are opening a "GOGI Honor Dorm" and 40 women who agreed to study GOGI and become GOGI Peer Coaches were moved into this building to begin their training.

Officer Valenzuela approached Maria. "I think you would be a good GOGI leader," Officer Valenzuela said. "I am in charge of filling the last two bunks. Do you want to go?" Maria has just read about BELLY BREATHING. She feels her chest tighten with the pressure of the decisions.

Officer Valenzuela is a new kind of officer. She has been trained in GOGI and knows how to speak to prisoners who are using the GOGI Tools. She pauses for a moment, letting the invitation sink into Maria's thoughts.

"Listen. You can do things like you have always done, or you can do something different. Do a little BELLY BREATHING. Stand right here and I will be back in a few moments. Remember you have BOSS OF MY BRAIN and you have BELLY BREATHING now, and, if you go to the GOGI Honor Dorm, you will learn more. I'll be right back."

Let's say that you can stand right next to Maria and remind her of BOSS OF MY BRAIN. What would you say to her, if she were willing to review BOSS OF MY BRAIN with you?

____

____

Let's say she is still listening and you continue with BELLY BREATHING, how might you help her remember this tool as she makes her decision? ______________________

____

____

All of a sudden the alarms ring and all prisoners are ordered to drop to the ground. Officers are running everywhere trying to break up a fight on the yard between two women. Everyone is returned to their cells or dorms and the entire yard is on lockdown.

Maria is angry and does not hesitate to voice her opinion about the women fighting, everyone being punished, and Officer Valenzuela leaving her shift without moving her and how the system is messed up.

What do you say to Maria? How can you encourage her to use her tools while she patiently awaits the opportunity to speak with Officer Valenzuela once again? ______________________

____

____

____

____

INCREASING MY PEACE – ACCOUNTABILITY BOX

DO YOU WANT CREDIT FOR THIS COURSE? REMEMBER TO KEEP TRACK OF YOUR DAILY STUDY BY COMPLETING THE INFORMATION BELOW TO GET YOUR CREDIT.

The month is________________; The day is ______________; The year is________; Solo study or group? ___________

Day 5 – BREATHING LIKE A BABY

When babies enter this world it is to their advantage to be born into a peaceful environment free of drugs or violence. Unfortunately, too often babies are not born in an environment that is necessarily safe or secure. These babies oftentimes do not learn how to breathe using their entire body. When a baby feels safe and secure, the baby's entire body will expand and contract with every breath.

When you were a baby, do you think you learned how to breathe using your entire body? Or do you think you might not have been in a safe or secure environment? ______________________________

____

____

____

Even if you were born in the most wonderful home, it is inevitable that at some point as a baby you got frightened or scared of something. In that moment, your breath became shallow, or you held your breath.

Can you remember a time when, as a child, you were frightened and you held your breath or your breathing was shallow and frightened? ____

____

*Is it possible that holding your breath or not breathing fully became more common than relaxed breathing as a result of experiences in your childhood?*___________________________________

____

____

Today, as you end the day and lay on your bunk, place one hand on your belly and one hand on your chest and observe how quickly your breathing becomes BELLY BREATHING. Did your body relax quickly or did it take a lot of time to have BELLY BREATHING take over? __________________

____

____

____

Can you see a link between relaxing and being more peaceful? How are they linked? ___________

____

____

____

____

INCREASING MY PEACE – ACCOUNTABILITY BOX

DO YOU WANT CREDIT FOR THIS COURSE? REMEMBER TO KEEP TRACK OF YOUR DAILY STUDY BY COMPLETING THE INFORMATION BELOW TO GET YOUR CREDIT.

The month is________________; The day is ______________; The year is________; Solo study or group? ____________

LIFE HAPPENS

It was only a week after being moved to the GOGI Honor Dorm that Maria was assigned to lead a group study on BELLY BREATHING. She knows she is not a teacher or leader type and feels like a big phony. Everyone else in the GOGI Honor Dorm really believes change is possible but for Maria, the new housing is only appealing because they get microwaves and a bigger television screen in the dayroom.

"Come on, Maria," her bunkie breaks the silence in their room. "You just have been a big downer ever since you were assigned to lead the group. Wassup?"

Maria is tempted to lie because that is just how she has operated her entire life. Instead, she puts one hand on her belly and feels the air getting into her stomach area. "BELLY BREATHING, that's what's up," she replies.

Her bunkie smiles and nods approvingly.

Knowing what you know about Maria, what might be going through her head right now? ________

____

____

____

____

What might she be thinking about herself? ______________________________

____

____

What is she thinking about being in the GOGI Honor Dorm and being required to lead a study group?

____

____

____

Write down what you think she can do to feel a little more comfortable in this new world where she has put herself. How can she become more comfortable? Do you think Maria will ever "change" enough so that she does not feel so miserable and out of place all the time? __________________

____

____

____

____

INCREASING MY PEACE – ACCOUNTABILITY BOX

DO YOU WANT CREDIT FOR THIS COURSE? REMEMBER TO KEEP TRACK OF YOUR DAILY STUDY BY COMPLETING THE INFORMATION BELOW TO GET YOUR CREDIT.

The month is__________________; The day is ________________; The year is_________; Solo study or group? ____________

Day 6 – BELLY BREATHING - A POWERFUL CRIME STOPPER

GOGI receives hundreds of letters each month from students who state the benefits of their GOGI Tools. Frequently, a GOGI student will state that if they had BELLY BREATHING as a tool they would not be serving time in prison, because they would not have committed the crime that got them locked up.

Why do you think that there are prisoners across the United State of America that state they would not have committed their crime if they had been taught BELLY BREATHING as a child? _________

____

____

What is your explanation? Why do they say BELLY BREATHING could have stopped them from committing a crime? ____

____

____

While it might be difficult in a heated moment to slow down enough to actually consider how you are breathing, with enough practice, you can build into your life a constant reminder to check your breathing to make sure you are getting oxygen into your body. Some of the most angry and violent individuals have found great levels of peace and power with BELLY BREATHING, and their anger no longer controls them.

How might you practice BELLY BREATHING each day so it becomes part of the way that you operate in the world? What do you think you need to do to have BELLY BREATHING be part of who you are?

____

____

When you become aware of BELLY BREATHING it will be easy for you to look at others and see if they are BELLY BREATHING or not. You will see that leaders, peaceful people, successful people, and those who seem the happiest are those who breathe with their entire body. You will also see that those who are constantly in or causing trouble are not really as happy as they pretend to be, nor are they peaceful. What they all have in common is the lack of good breathing.

Observe others today. Do you notice people who naturally do BELLY BREATHING? Do they seem calm and in control? When you observe hotheads or angry people, do they breathe properly? _____

____

If someone were to observe you, what would they say about your breathing? _________________

____

____

INCREASING MY PEACE – ACCOUNTABILITY BOX

DO YOU WANT CREDIT FOR THIS COURSE? REMEMBER TO KEEP TRACK OF YOUR DAILY STUDY BY COMPLETING THE INFORMATION BELOW TO GET YOUR CREDIT.

The month is__________________; The day is ________________; The year is_________; Solo study or group? ______________

LIFE HAPPENS

AdSeg again. Maria couldn't handle the responsibility that came with being in the GOGI Honor dorm so she sabotaged her success by stealing her bunkie's commissary. She knew exactly what she was doing when she did it and now her attitude is worse than it has ever been.

She is officially in the F-it mode and resigned to always living in and out of feeling like a total loser. Of course, she blames her bunkie; she has consistently used this tactic to play the convenient role of victim.

Let's say you are the counselor assigned to assessing Maria and her mental state so you can move her to the housing most appropriate for her needs. If you were the counselor, what questions might you ask? ____

____

____

*If you were a counselor who was trained in GOGI Tools, what questions might you ask her about her tools?*____

____

____

"Yeah, counselor," Maria says, "The GOGI Tools are all fine and dandy, but they don't help when you don't believe in yourself. If you have always been low, low is just where you are going to remain."

*What is your reply?*____

____

____

"How would you know?" Maria says. "You have a high paid counselor position, you don't know anything about my life. How can I believe YOU?" Based on your real life experience, what would you tell Maria? ____

____

____

____

Do you see the value of your life experience in helping others? Why are people who have overcome obstacles more believable than those who have not had a similar struggle? ____________________

____

____

____

INCREASING MY PEACE – ACCOUNTABILITY BOX

DO YOU WANT CREDIT FOR THIS COURSE? REMEMBER TO KEEP TRACK OF YOUR DAILY STUDY BY COMPLETING THE INFORMATION BELOW TO GET YOUR CREDIT.

The month is______________; The day is ______________; The year is________; Solo study or group? ________

Day 7 – Recap and Review

Write the STATEMENT OF PURPOSE AND OWNERSHIP for BELLY BREATHING. __________

What are the keywords for BELLY BREATHING? __________

What do you like about BELLY BREATHING? __________

How might BELLY BREATHING help you in making the most positive decisions? __________

What does "stress can be your friend" mean to you? __________

What does 'stress' or 'loss aversion' mean to you? __________

How might BELLY BREATHING be used as a "crime stopper?" __________

What does "one hand on your belly" mean to you? __________

Ultimate Freedom
GOGI
ART BY : ARMANDO "SANDOVAL" 2015

INCREASING MY PEACE – ACCOUNTABILITY BOX

DO YOU WANT CREDIT FOR THIS COURSE? REMEMBER TO KEEP TRACK OF YOUR DAILY STUDY BY COMPLETING THE INFORMATION BELOW TO GET YOUR CREDIT.

The month is_______________; The day is _______________; The year is________; Solo study or group? __________

YOUR PEACE PAGE

This page is provided for you to answer questions you may eventually be asked about your anger and your ability to choose another response.

Humans usually choose anger, rage, and violence when they are not aware of more positive options. Sometimes it feels as if there is no other option. At one time in your past did you ever feel that you had no choice but anger? Why? ____

____

____

As you think about the times in your life when you got angry and this resulted in actions that you may now regret, please write about your choices at that time.

____

____

____

Did you not know you had a choice? Was a peaceful choice too difficult? Was a peaceful choice impossible? ____

____

____

____

Given what you have learned so far in this course, what would have been different? ___________

____

____

____

*What choices did you have?*____

____

____

What tools might have helped you make a peaceful choice? __________________________

____

____

____

INCREASING MY PEACE – ACCOUNTABILITY BOX

DO YOU WANT CREDIT FOR THIS COURSE? REMEMBER TO KEEP TRACK OF YOUR DAILY STUDY BY COMPLETING THE INFORMATION BELOW TO GET YOUR CREDIT.

The month is________________; The day is ______________; The year is________; Solo study or group? ____________

YOUR STRATEGY PAGE

This page is provided for you to answer questions you may eventually be asked about strategies you have for your future. Start to formalize a plan so that when life serves up its inevitable challenges, you are prepared to handle them by INCREASING YOUR PEACE.

What will you do if you can't find employment? ______________________________

____

What will you do if your home life takes a turn for the worse? ______________________

____

____

What will you do when tempted to return to the poor decision-making that landed you in the hands of a corrections department? ______________________________

____

____

Humans are always more successful when they practice and plan how to handle things. When humans are unprepared or have not practiced or planned, they are often less successful than those who DO practice and plan.

As you plan for success, how can INCREASING YOUR PEACE help you in your plan for success? __

____

How can increasing your peace help you with the following:

Home: ____

____

Work: ____

____

Money: ____

____

Spiritual practice: ____

____

Physical health: ____

____

Obligations and duties: ____

____

INCREASING MY PEACE – ACCOUNTABILITY BOX

DO YOU WANT CREDIT FOR THIS COURSE? REMEMBER TO KEEP TRACK OF YOUR DAILY STUDY BY COMPLETING THE INFORMATION BELOW TO GET YOUR CREDIT.

The month is________________; The day is ______________; The year is________; Solo study or group? __________

DEEP DIVING - Getting to the bottom of it

If you had learned options to anger as a child, what are a few things that could be different in your life right now? ________________________________

____

____

*If you were to live every day for the rest of your life with no anger, but solid options for reacting to irritating situations, what might be different for you?*________________________________

____

____

____

If you were to repeatedly practice the tools taught to you in this course, do you believe your life would benefit? If so, how? If not, what would it take for you to improve your life experience?

____

____

____

____

There are many benefits to increasing your peace. In your own words, what might be the benefit to you and those you love if you were a person at peace with life and others? ________________

____

____

____

____

You have read quite a bit of material in this workbook so far. What has been the most impactful and why? ________________________________

____

____

____

____

____

INCREASING MY PEACE – ACCOUNTABILITY BOX

DO YOU WANT CREDIT FOR THIS COURSE? REMEMBER TO KEEP TRACK OF YOUR DAILY STUDY BY COMPLETING THE INFORMATION BELOW TO GET YOUR CREDIT.

The month is__________________; The day is ________________; The year is________; Solo study or group? ____________

DEEP DIVING

Use these pages to write down how you might describe your own rehabilitation, or how to explain to a loved one how you are no longer the person you once were. However you use these pages, let them reflect your insight, your understanding, and your ability to be the best person you can be.

Can you perceive yourself as someone who is loved for the peace and contentment others feel when they are around you? What would that feel like? ______________________________________

____

____

____

____

Do you know anyone who makes you feel at peace when they are around? What are the qualities they have that let you feel a level of peace? ______________________________________

____

____

Do you respect them? Why? ______________________________________

____

____

Do you know people who always seem angry? Is it pleasant to be around those people, or does it create stress in those who are nearby? ______________________________________

____

____

____

____

If our stress and anger level directly impacts the lives of others, can this be motivation for you to increase your peace? ______________________________________

____

____

____

____

This is art is a gift to GOGI from Keith E.

INCREASING MY PEACE – ACCOUNTABILITY BOX

DO YOU WANT CREDIT FOR THIS COURSE? REMEMBER TO KEEP TRACK OF YOUR DAILY STUDY BY COMPLETING THE INFORMATION BELOW TO GET YOUR CREDIT.

The month is________________; The day is ________________; The year is________; Solo study or group? ____________

Week 3

INCREASING YOUR PEACE WITH FIVE SECOND LIGHTSWITCH

To study the same tool as all other GOGI students, you may wish to study this chapter on:
3rd Week of January
3rd Week of April
3rd Week of July
3rd Week of October

PREPARING TO SUCCEED THIS WEEK

In this book or other GOGI materials, read the sections that mention the GOGI FIVE SECOND LIGHTSWITCH. Reading these sections of the book will give you great power to understand and apply this tool immediately in your life. You will also do better in your coursework when you read more about the tool in your GOGI books.

What is the title of the GOGI book or books you have to study this week's tool? ________________

____

*On what pages did you find information about FIVE SECOND LIGHTSWITCH?*________________

____

What are the keywords for FIVE SECOND LIGHTSWITCH? ____________________________

____

*What did you read that interested you?*______________________________________

____

According to the GOGI Calendar, which weeks of the year do most GOGI students study FIVE SECOND LIGHTSWITCH? ____________________________________

____

____

What do you like, personally, about FIVE SECOND LIGHTSWITCH? ________________

____

____

____

____

INCREASING MY PEACE – ACCOUNTABILITY BOX

DO YOU WANT CREDIT FOR THIS COURSE? REMEMBER TO KEEP TRACK OF YOUR DAILY STUDY BY COMPLETING THE INFORMATION BELOW TO GET YOUR CREDIT.

The month is________________; The day is ______________; The year is__________; Solo study or group? ____________

Have you read about these tools in this book yet? If not, you are cheating yourself of important information that will help you be the best version of you. Before you start with this week's study, please do yourself a favor and take a moment to read about these tools in this and other GOGI books. Then, continue with today's study.

Day 1 – UNDER NEW CONSTRUCTION

The FIVE SECOND LIGHTSWITCH tool was created by prisoners, of course, but this particular tool was explained best by a prisoner who had a career in construction and was an expert in the electrical wiring of homes.

Someone in a GOGI study group stated that when his anger or drug use started to take hold that it seemed as if he had no control, that the anger or drug use just "happened" before he realized it. It seemed automatic.

The experienced construction worker tried to explain FIVE SECOND LIGHTSWITCH to the guy. He said that FIVE SECOND LIGHTSWITCH would help him create a "new wire" and lead all that energy to a more productive result. He told him that anger was just an old wire to an old habit and that he could simply reconstruct the wire and send it in a different direction.

He stated that in construction he could connect a switch, a wire, and a light bulb. He also stated that if he didn't like that light he could redirect the wire to light up somewhere else.

When you think of anger like part of a construction project, would you want your own old wire of anger to go to a new place? If you could redirect that wire of anger, where would you rather it lead to? ____

____

____

Some children grew up seeing parents enraged or acting violent. For others they came to think that violence means power. That anger means control. The fact that some people use violence as power does not mean it is the only way to handle a situation. The fact that some people use anger to control does not mean it is the only way to control a situation. There are many options in addition to violence. Violence is one option, not the only option. There are many options rather than anger. Anger is one option, not the only option. What is interesting is that we often act the way we saw adults act in our childhood and communities. Does that mean it is the only option?

*What was your own experience of anger and/or violence when you were young? Is there a belief that you might be perceived as "weak" if you do not act out with anger or violence?*______________

____

____

____

____

DO YOU WANT CREDIT FOR THIS COURSE? REMEMBER TO KEEP TRACK OF YOUR DAILY STUDY BY COMPLETING THE INFORMATION BELOW TO GET YOUR CREDIT.

The month is________________; The day is ________________; The year is________; Solo study or group? ____________

LIFE HAPPENS

Jerome knew violence all too well. He was smacked upside the head as a kid too many times to remember. His mom raised him the best she could but getting a whoopin' was the only way she could control him. Then there were the guys she had moving in and out of his life and their apartment. They were always hitting her for one reason or the next. Eventually, he started hitting them so they would stop hitting her. Hitting was just what you did when someone did something you didn't like.

Jerome got really good at controlling others with the menacing glare he learned from his mom. And since he had taken so many punches in his life, getting hit was not a worry for him. He would hit anyone, any size, and for any reason.

"What is another option if hitting someone is not one of them?" a prisoner in the GOGI study group asked of Jerome.

"I dunno. When you hit someone they stop," Jerome replied. "I am not going to look weak by letting someone get away with somethin'," he added.

If Jerome was in your GOGI study group, what options might you give him that are actually realistic options rather than unrealistic things he would never do? ________________________

Knowing the kind of childhood Jerome had, knowing that violence was just the norm, how can you let him know that violence may have been HIS norm, but it was not THE ONLY NORM? What would you say? ________________________

Jerome listens to you. He respects your take on things. You decide to tell him about "reconstruction" of his habits and "rewiring" habits that you learned from the construction worker that compared old habits to old wiring in a house. How do you describe to Jerome that violence and anger are old wiring that can be swapped out? What would you say to him to get him to understand that he can create new wiring in his mind? ________________________

INCREASING MY PEACE – ACCOUNTABILITY BOX

DO YOU WANT CREDIT FOR THIS COURSE? REMEMBER TO KEEP TRACK OF YOUR DAILY STUDY BY COMPLETING THE INFORMATION BELOW TO GET YOUR CREDIT.

The month is____________________; The day is __________________; The year is__________; Solo study or group? _______________

Day 2 – DON'T STOP - JUST FLIP THE SWITCH

Imagine a freeway filled with cars. Let's say a truck overturns and traffic comes to a halt with some cars running into each other and others barely avoiding a collision. The drivers of all the hundreds of cars stuck on the freeway get irritated while they wait for the truck to be moved aside. Eventually the rush of traffic resumes down the same road, cars picking up speed, and everyone is even more anxious to get to their intended destination.

Trying to STOP anger is similar to stopping traffic on a freeway. It usually just sits there waiting for the opportunity to rev the engines once again.

FIVE SECOND LIGHTSWITCH works well for anger because it diverts the traffic off the freeway of your old bad habit. With FIVE SECOND LIGHTSWITCH the truck might topple over, but within five seconds all the traffic heads to the nearest off-ramp and peacefully towards a new and better direction.

FIVE SECOND LIGHTSWITCH is your off-ramp, away from the pending wreck.

When you think about anger and violence like a freeway pile-up, is it easier to see that finding an off-ramp might be beneficial? Why? ____

____

____

____

When you think of all the times you simply "tried" to stop your anger, and somehow it only got bottled-up and got bigger, does it make sense now, when you think of it like a freeway of emotions? Stopping the traffic is only temporary, getting the traffic off the freeway of emotion is a simple solution. How might this knowledge help you in the future when you might get angry, frustrated, or enraged? ____

____

____

____

____

If a fellow GOGI student were to tell you that they have bottled-up anger or that they are always angry, how might you describe for them how having a FIVE SECOND LIGHTSWITCH will help them divert the traffic in their mind? What would you say? __________________________________

____

____

____

____

INCREASING MY PEACE – ACCOUNTABILITY BOX

DO YOU WANT CREDIT FOR THIS COURSE? REMEMBER TO KEEP TRACK OF YOUR DAILY STUDY BY COMPLETING THE INFORMATION BELOW TO GET YOUR CREDIT.

The month is________________; The day is ______________; The year is________; Solo study or group? ____________

LIFE HAPPENS

Let's check in with one of JJ's old cellies. From a prior week we met, Marco. Sure enough, the C.O. of the building rushes over and tells Marco to put his hands up on the wall. Without resistance, Marco is cuffed and headed to Administrative Segregation for slamming the phone down so hard that it qualified as an attempt to bust up state property. (The poor phones in that unit.) You know what that means. It's a write-up in his C-file, something that could possibly alter the course of Marco's wish to get out of this place.

You watched the entire thing, play by play. First, Marco started the call while he was agitated because his team just lost the Super Bowl. He was not being the BOSS OF HIS BRAIN. He was running through a lot of emotions. The EMOTIONAL PART of his brain took over by the third quarter of the game and it never let up. Then, instead of using his BELLY BREATHING, you watched from your cell window as Marco started what looked like hyperventilating as he raised his voice louder and louder. At this point you also noticed the C.O. taking notice and just waiting to see what Marco would do next.

When Marco let rip a dozen or more cuss words you knew it was a done deal and he would be spending the night in Administrative Segregation. Then the futile attempt to bust the phone occurred and you knew the potential prized GOGI student had just reverted back to his old ways and tossed out all your teachings in a matter of 30 seconds.

Sitting on your bunk you are more than a little discouraged. Why didn't you do a better job as a Peer Coach? Did you miss something? Why do you think Marco spun out of control so quickly? ________

____

____

What might you have done to help him prepare a little better for times when he got angry? _______

____

____

Some GOGI students help others by having them write out different scenarios and then write a plan for how they might respond. Would you do that with Marco next time? ____________________

____

____

When dealing with your own anger and temper issues, what are some situations where you think you might be tempted to react in an old and unmanageable way? ____________________

____

Do you think that planning ahead how you will respond could be helpful to you? ____________

____

____

INCREASING MY PEACE – ACCOUNTABILITY BOX

DO YOU WANT CREDIT FOR THIS COURSE? REMEMBER TO KEEP TRACK OF YOUR DAILY STUDY BY COMPLETING THE INFORMATION BELOW TO GET YOUR CREDIT.

The month is________________; The day is ______________; The year is________; Solo study or group? __________

Day 3 – FIVE FINGER REMINDER

When anger starts to boil up inside you, it might seem a little messy and more than impossible to stop yourself and start thinking about GOGI Tools. Maybe that is why one GOGI student decided to create her own FIVE SECOND LIGHTSWITCH. Instead of trying to remember her tool, she would realize when she was headed down an old road and she would hold out her hand and look at her fingers. Her name is Teri and she went from living under a freeway with a needle in her arm, to a respectable daughter and mother – totally and completely in sober service of her family.

For Teri to understand FIVE SECOND LIGHTSWITCH she assigned each finger on her hand a good reason for her to do a POSITIVE ACTION. Each finger represented one of her children. When she was headed down a dark road she simply named her children by looking at each finger and saying their names out loud. Then she found it easier to get to her POSITIVE ACTION.

Another GOGI student gave each of his fingers his own reason for getting to a POSITIVE ACTION. His sobriety, his sanity, his future, his reputation, and his God.

If you were to use your fingers to remind you to flip your FIVE SECOND LIGHTSWITCH, what would five good reasons be for you to get to your POSITIVE ACTION as quickly as possible? ____________

____

____

One other GOGI student simply touched his thumb with each finger and that, to him, was all he needed before he looked for a glass of water. Drinking a glass of water was his POSITIVE ACTION, and the one thing he would always try to do when he wanted something more productive than his old go-to anger and temper tantrums.

In deciding what your POSITIVE ACTION might be, what are some simple things you could have ready and waiting? Would drinking water work for you? Reading? Walking? Sit-ups? Writing a letter? What might your action be?

How might you remember to FLIP THE SWITCH? ______________________________

____

What might be the biggest obstacle to getting to your POSITIVE ACTION? ______________

____

____

How might you best remind yourself that you have FIVE SECOND LIGHTSWITCH? __________

____

____

____

INCREASING MY PEACE – ACCOUNTABILITY BOX

DO YOU WANT CREDIT FOR THIS COURSE? REMEMBER TO KEEP TRACK OF YOUR DAILY STUDY BY COMPLETING THE INFORMATION BELOW TO GET YOUR CREDIT.

The month is_________________; The day is _______________; The year is________; Solo study or group? ______________

LIFE HAPPENS

It turns out that Jerome and Marco end up as friends. They both seem to be doing pretty well these days and you have actually seen them sitting in the dayroom with two other guys reading one of the new GOGI books.

Jerome comes up to you. "Hey, Marco and me, well, we are doin' this GOGI thing in the dayroom and it's my turn to kinda lead next week and I am not real clear on the FIVE SECOND LIGHTSWITCH thing. Can you explain it to me in plain English?"

First off, you are more than a little irritated. You were the one to bring GOGI to the building and now Marco, Jerome, and two other guys are doing GOGI without you. You are about ready to tell Jerome off, but you realize that Jerome and Marco can do whatever they want. You realize that you do not own the GOGI Tools, but they are there for everyone. Rather than cut him down, you remember BOSS OF MY BRAIN and you get all the thinking to the smart part.

"Here's the thing, Jerome. You don't need to be an expert in GOGI Tools to share them. GOGI was designed by and for prisoners. We share and explore with others. Your best bet is to speak from your experience, where you have seen it work in your life," you say.

Jerome thinks for a second. "Well, from my experience, you are the only one who knows these GOGI Tools backwards and forwards. I will use you as my example and just tell them how you got me to see I could use the tools, too," Jerome says with a smile.

How might the scenario have turned out differently if you would have told Jerome you didn't appreciate him running off and doing his own thing? ____

____

Does knowing the tools "backwards and forwards" make you immune to actions and reactions of the past? Is just knowledge enough or is there something else that is needed? __________________

____

GOGI believes that the finest leaders are those who inspire others to lead as well. How does this scenario show growth and leadership? ____

____

What are some other things that you could do to further inspire Marco and Jerome as they build positive social support for their continued self-improvement? __________________________

____

A few weeks later, Marco approaches you and states that his family has seen a difference in him and he wants to thank you. Without you, he would not be speaking to his son again. There seems to be a tear in Marco's eye when he says this to you. How do you respond? ____________________

____

INCREASING MY PEACE – ACCOUNTABILITY BOX

DO YOU WANT CREDIT FOR THIS COURSE? REMEMBER TO KEEP TRACK OF YOUR DAILY STUDY BY COMPLETING THE INFORMATION BELOW TO GET YOUR CREDIT.

The month is________________; The day is ______________; The year is________; Solo study or group? __________

Day 4 – OLD THOUGHT? NEW ACTION!

Your brain is a very powerful machine that you probably have not used to your full advantage. Much of what you do has probably become automatic and it may feel beyond your control. This is especially true with addictions. The brain believes that you want more and so it locks into full force getting you more of what it thinks you want. Anger, too, can be addicting. It can become something your brain honestly believes you want to create. Can you change this? Yes, you can. It is not easy, but it is probable with GOGI Tools. Prisoners created FIVE SECOND LIGHTSWITCH because addictions are oftentimes at the root of incarceration. When humans are free from their addictions, they usually don't commit crimes.

What do you think about the statement that when humans are free from their addictions they usually don't commit crimes? What does that mean to you? ______________________________

____

____

Why do you think anger can be addicting to some people? Have you known someone or are you someone where anger seems to pop up without forethought or thinking about consequences? ______

____

____

Why do you think it might not be easy to FLIP THE SWITCH and get to a NEW ACTION? Why is it easy to read but hard to do? ______________________________________

____

The key in using FIVE SECOND LIGHTSWITCH is not to try to stop the thought, because that does not work for most humans. Rather than trying to stop the thought, you need to realize you have the thought, then act as quickly as you can before five seconds is up and get to your preplanned POSITIVE ACTION.

OLD THOUGHT? NEW ACTION!

Why is a NEW ACTION important? Because your brain needs to focus on what you are doing. Your brain will be thinking, "Oh. OK. You don't want to get mad right now, you really want to get a glass of water. Ok. We can do water. Let's go get a glass of water." This short break in your brain's focus permits you to use your other tools to train your brain that the old way is no way. ____________

____

____

What can you do to help yourself be the boss over your reactions rather than the victim of an old habit that never really worked for you anyway? What POSITIVE ACTIONS might be proactive in gaining power over the past? ______________________________________

____

DO YOU WANT CREDIT FOR THIS COURSE? REMEMBER TO KEEP TRACK OF YOUR DAILY STUDY BY COMPLETING THE INFORMATION BELOW TO GET YOUR CREDIT.

The month is________________; The day is ______________; The year is________; Solo study or group? ____________

LIFE HAPPENS

Your new cellie is a good guy. He is taking it hard that he got handed down an LWOP (life without parole) sentence a year ago. He will tell you straight up he is guilty. He killed the man - and the woman - and he ran, stole the car, shot at the cops, he lied, yelled at the judge, beat up a Deputy in the Sheriff's department, and spit at the Corrections Officer. He is the first one to tell you he has always had an anger problem. The problem is, that is all he will tell you. He goes on and on about how guilty he is, how he destroyed his life, how his anger is always out of control, how he destroyed his mother, he destroyed his wife, he will never see his kids. You have heard it a million times before. You know it is important to let a guy sit with his situation for a while. You know that, but it's been a year now and something must shift.

Using your skills with your GOGI Tools, what might you tell this guy? How might you get his OLD THOUGHT to a NEW ACTION and help him FLIP THE SWITCH? ______________________

____

____

Does his story of out of control anger sound familiar to you? Do you know someone or are you someone that has experienced anger that seemed out of control? What information do you wish someone would have shared with you? ______________________________________

____

____

Redirecting the thought is the first step to taking the power back over your life. A distraction often works to get the mind out of a rut and headed into a positive direction. This distraction is best when created internally, but an external distraction might help to get the process started.

*You know your new cellie does not know that he can redirect his thoughts so you ask if he wouldn't mind if you read out loud and asked him some questions. He agrees and you pull out your GOGI book. What part of the GOGI materials do you think might be helpful to him?*______________

____

____

____

*When you get into a rut, what are some of the things that help you redirect your thoughts?*________

____

____

____

____

INCREASING MY PEACE – ACCOUNTABILITY BOX

DO YOU WANT CREDIT FOR THIS COURSE? REMEMBER TO KEEP TRACK OF YOUR DAILY STUDY BY COMPLETING THE INFORMATION BELOW TO GET YOUR CREDIT.

The month is________________; The day is ________________; The year is________; Solo study or group? __________

Day 5 - FLIP THE SWITCH

Most people with anger or violence in their history will tell you that there comes a point where there is "no turning back," a time when things have gone too far. Some people even say that they don't remember doing something violent, that they "black out" or simply "don't remember" the results of anger or rage. It was best described by one GOGI student who stated that he went from "A to Z with no letters inbetween."

This GOGI student is not uncommon. For many of us, the distance between anger and a regrettable action seems very condensed. Maybe that is why a prisoner helped create FIVE SECOND LIGHTSWITCH. He claimed that if he could FLIP THE SWITCH then the distance from A to Z had many options. Specifically, if he got to a POSITIVE ACTION before five seconds had gone by, then all was good.

Was there a time recently when you wish you could have FLIPPED THE SWITCH and directed all your energy in a more positive direction? Briefly write down one time when FLIPPING THE SWITCH could have kept you from an angry or violent reaction. ____________________

____

____

____

FIVE SECOND LIGHTSWITCH asks you to FLIP THE SWITCH to a POSITIVE ACTION within five seconds. If you are in the chow line and someone makes you really angry, what might be two or three actions you might use to avoid confrontation? ____________________

____

If you are in your cell and you are not let out for yard because the new C.O. doesn't give anyone enough time to get dressed, what are two or three actions you can do to keep anger from building up inside you? ____________________

____

____

When it comes to moving your OLD THOUGHT to a NEW ACTION, where do you believe you will have the most challenge? With people who have power over you? With family who may be making some bad decisions? With a 'friend' who lies or cheats at your expense?

What are three situations where getting to a NEW ACTION will be the greatest challenge?

1) ____

2) ____

3) ____

DO YOU WANT CREDIT FOR THIS COURSE? REMEMBER TO KEEP TRACK OF YOUR DAILY STUDY BY COMPLETING THE INFORMATION BELOW TO GET YOUR CREDIT.

The month is________________; The day is ______________; The year is________; Solo study or group? ____________

LIFE HAPPENS

You are asked to speak to a college psychology class that is scheduled to tour your prison. You will be representing your entire building, and you were voted into this opportunity by the men in your building. You know this is an honor and you don't want to disappoint the men or the students.

It is one hour before the event. Your clothes are pressed and you are reviewing your introduction speech and feeling anxious but in a very good way. Just then, the yard alarms go off and you start hearing the telltale signs of trouble. This time it takes longer than usual to quiet things down and you know the longer there is a ruckus the longer the lockdown is likely to be. You are hoping beyond all hope that the tour will still happen...but, alas, the tour is canceled. The yard is on lockdown. Again.

What GOGI Tool will you use in this situation and why? ______________________________

____

____

How can you best prepare to share with the students what they might need to know to help the perception of prisoners change? ______________________________

____

____

How can you be a part of the solution? How can you help the men realize the need for peace on the yard? ______________________________

____

*How can you tell them that until violence is not an option, that prisons will continue to hold back prisoners? How do you help the men on this yard realize that when violence is replaced by peaceful resolution, prisons will change?*______________________________

____

____

How can you share with the prisoners that they are their own worst enemy? That the public is frightened of prisoners because of the violence that a small number of prisoners perpetuate? _____

____

And, most importantly, how do you deal with your own disappointment? ______________________________

____

____

____

____

INCREASING MY PEACE – ACCOUNTABILITY BOX

DO YOU WANT CREDIT FOR THIS COURSE? REMEMBER TO KEEP TRACK OF YOUR DAILY STUDY BY COMPLETING THE INFORMATION BELOW TO GET YOUR CREDIT.

The month is________________; The day is ______________; The year is________; Solo study or group? __________

Day 6 – THE POWER IN PEACE

Some free people argue that prisoners say they want the system to change, but prisoners must also participate in the development of a new way to exist in prison settings. Some state that in prison there is a belief that you are weak if you don't use violence to solve a problem. Some people believe that peaceful prisoners are bullied by the few who wield violence in the yard. Free people will argue that this is a belief and this culture is what keeps prisoners in prison; it keeps prisoners weak and at the mercy of the law and those who wear a badge.

What do you think about this perception that by permitting violence, prisoners are keeping themselves trapped? Is it possible for a prisoner to be strong and not resort to violence? How? _____

____

____

____

____

When violence breaks out on a prison yard, everyone on that yard pays the price for the act of violence. What might prisoners do to support and encourage peaceful resolutions to problems? How might prisoners be at the forefront of the change they want within the prison system? __________

____

____

____

____

In dealing with your own anger, how can gaining power over your anger and developing the strength of peace help all other prisoners? How can you change your own "culture" and your own way of handling problems? ________________________________

____

____

____

How can being in power over your anger help your family? How can being in power over your anger help children? ________________________________

____

____

____

____

DO YOU WANT CREDIT FOR THIS COURSE? REMEMBER TO KEEP TRACK OF YOUR DAILY STUDY BY COMPLETING THE INFORMATION BELOW TO GET YOUR CREDIT.

The month is________________; The day is _______________; The year is________; Solo study or group? ____________

LIFE HAPPENS

Your cellie comes back from seeing the counselor and appears happy. His first bit of news is that his transfer is in full motion and he will be moved closer to his family. You are happy for him, even though your heart aches a little. You have not seen your family since the last glance you caught as you were taken out of the courtroom more than ten years ago. Since then, your mom has died, your sister moved to Chicago with some guy who won't let her write to you, and your brother is – you hear – in some Federal prison for breaking into post office boxes and taking credit cards to feed his drug habit.

How do you deal with the rush of feelings you get when something good happens for someone else and you feel stuck? How do you FLIP THE SWITCH so your mind does not travel too far down a dark road? ____

____

____

____

Then you are pushed over the edge. He tells you that the counselor signed him up for a GOGI workshop and that the GOGI Coaches are coming to the prison and she added him to the list.

"What list?" you ask.

"Don't blame me, bro," he replies. "I don't know nothin' bout this GOGI thing other than what you tell me. She asked if I wanted to go and I said sure."

Now your blood starts to boil. YOU are the one who wrote GOGI asking if they could come do a workshop to start GOGI at your prison. YOU are the one who has been sharing GOGI with all the men. You are the one who even purchased a book with your hard-earned money because the prison didn't have ONE book! How could there be a workshop and your cellie gets in and you are left out?

What do you do? How do you feel and what do you do with those feelings of frustration and – yep – downright ANGER! ____

____

____

Life can be – and usually is – unfair. Sometimes those who don't deserve things get handed them on a silver platter. How do you handle the anger that comes from this little piece of reality? How do you INCREASE YOUR PEACE inside you so you don't act out and create a worse situation? How can FIVE SECOND LIGHTSWITCH play a part in your internal peace? ____________________

____

____

____

INCREASING MY PEACE – ACCOUNTABILITY BOX

DO YOU WANT CREDIT FOR THIS COURSE? REMEMBER TO KEEP TRACK OF YOUR DAILY STUDY BY COMPLETING THE INFORMATION BELOW TO GET YOUR CREDIT.

The month is________________; The day is ______________; The year is________; Solo study or group? ____________

Day 7 – Recap and Review

Write the STATEMENT OF PURPOSE AND OWNERSHIP for FIVE SECOND LIGHTSWITCH. (Information about the GOGI Tool is found near the front of this course where the tools are described)

____

____

____

What are the keywords for FIVE SECOND LIGHTSWITCH? ____________________

____

____

What do you like about FIVE SECOND LIGHTSWITCH? ____________________

____

____

How might FIVE SECOND LIGHTSWITCH help you in making the most positive decisions? ______

____

When you think of FLIPPING THE SWITCH, what comes to mind? ____________________

____

____

What are the POSITIVE ACTIONS you can reach out to within five seconds of a negative thought?

____

____

____

In what five ways might FIVE SECOND LIGHTSWITCH help you to INCREASE YOUR PEACE?

1) ____

2) ____

3) ____

4) ____

5) ____

One of the biggest differences in my life as a direct result of studying the 12 tools of GOGI and taking this course is found in the decisions I make on a daily basis. I have the power and control of choice. I can think, act, and respond in a negative (emotional/old habit) way or in a positive (smart part) way. I understand now that it is always my choice. I have the tools to meet the challenges and difficulties of life. One of my biggest triggers is witnessing what I perceive to be an injustice. It gets my blood boiling and I seek to bring "justice" to them. I used to believe they needed to be punished for their injustice. Harm for harm. Now that I have learned the GOGI tools and have adopted them into my life I now seek to heal rather than harm and this can only be accomplished through the use of my GOGI tools (sometimes nearly all of them). I am a positive influence and role model for my community and I seek to be of service to others regardless of my environment. Hurt people, hurt people and healed people, heal people. GOGI has enabled me to get out of my self-created prison and allowed me to experience Ultimate Freedom. It is the best freedom one can ever experience. I am a powerful force that is moving forward in a positive direction and no longer the weak, hurt, depressed, lost, and fearful individual who was stuck in the muck of despair.

~ I am GOGI-4-LIFE!! ~

JASON YATES - PVSP 2016

INCREASING MY PEACE – ACCOUNTABILITY BOX

DO YOU WANT CREDIT FOR THIS COURSE? REMEMBER TO KEEP TRACK OF YOUR DAILY STUDY BY COMPLETING THE INFORMATION BELOW TO GET YOUR CREDIT.

The month is________________; The day is _______________; The year is________; Solo study or group? ____________

YOUR PEACE PAGE

This page is provided for you to answer questions you may eventually be asked about your anger and your ability to choose another response.

Humans usually choose anger, rage, and violence when they are not aware or taught options. Were you taught peace or anger as a child?

____

Who was your most impactful teacher? For good or bad? __________________________

____

How might BELLY BREATHING be linked to FIVE SECOND LIGHTSWITCH? ______________

____

____

We each have many things we regret saying or doing. In thinking back on one of these times, did you realize that you had options in your response? Why or why not? __________________________

____

____

How does BOSS OF MY BRAIN help you filter what you say when you are angry? ____________

____

____

Did you place yourself in a situation where you had no choice? Could you have done anything differently to get a more peaceful outcome? ________________________________

____

____

What are the names of the three tools you have learned?

1) ____

2) ____

3) ____

Which is your favorite and why? _____________________________________

____

____

INCREASING MY PEACE – ACCOUNTABILITY BOX

DO YOU WANT CREDIT FOR THIS COURSE? REMEMBER TO KEEP TRACK OF YOUR DAILY STUDY BY COMPLETING THE INFORMATION BELOW TO GET YOUR CREDIT.

The month is________________; The day is ________________; The year is________; Solo study or group? ____________

YOUR STRATEGY PAGE

This page is provided for you to answer questions you may eventually be asked about strategies you have for your future.

You are likely to face all sorts of situations in the future that demand high levels of internal peace. Here are some real scenarios shared by formerly incarcerated GOGI students. Write down how you would respond in each scenario.

You get a new job and something is stolen. You are blamed. You overhear someone saying, "you know he is an ex-con."

What do you think? ____

What are you feeling? ____

What are your actions? ____

You had thought it would be wonderful to have your physical freedom, but the stress is really getting you down. You can't stand your boss who is worse than any C.O. you ever met, your transition home is worse than a level three prison, you are paid peanuts but you have bills that require serious dollars.

What do you think? ____

What are you feeling? ____

What are your actions? ____

Which tools do you put to work? ____

INCREASING MY PEACE – ACCOUNTABILITY BOX

DO YOU WANT CREDIT FOR THIS COURSE? REMEMBER TO KEEP TRACK OF YOUR DAILY STUDY BY COMPLETING THE INFORMATION BELOW TO GET YOUR CREDIT.

The month is__________________; The day is ________________; The year is_________; Solo study or group? ____________

DEEP DIVING - Getting to the bottom of it

Each of the GOGI Tools probably reminds you of other advice you have received in the past. Write down similarities you find between the GOGI Tools and other things you have learned in the past.

What is GOGI similar to? ____

____

____

____

Learning tools to increase your peace may remind you of things you were taught in the past. Who in your life offered suggestions and advice when you were growing up? Did you appreciate or resent their suggestions? ____

____

*I was taught...*____

____

*The person who taught me was...*____

____

____

Are there individuals in your life that you wish would heed your advice? Why do you think they may resist your suggestions? Who and why? ____

____

____

____

____

Do you think that you have naturally matured enough to see situations differently? Does this maturity give you insight you didn't have as a youngster? ____

____

____

Some say that maturity can naturally increase your peace. What do you think about this statement?

____

____

INCREASING MY PEACE – ACCOUNTABILITY BOX

DO YOU WANT CREDIT FOR THIS COURSE? REMEMBER TO KEEP TRACK OF YOUR DAILY STUDY BY COMPLETING THE INFORMATION BELOW TO GET YOUR CREDIT.

The month is________________; The day is ______________; The year is________; Solo study or group? ____________

DEEP DIVING

Use these pages to write down how you might describe your own rehabilitation, or how to explain to a loved one how you are no longer the person you once were. However you use these pages, let them reflect your insight, your understanding, and your ability to be the best person you can be.

What has been your process for "rehabilitation" during the past five years? ____________________

____

____

____

____

What is your intended outcome for your life? How do you want your life to unfold? ______________

____

____

____

____

Many GOGI students say they are less angry when they are helping others. What do you think that means? And, could that work for you? ______________________________

____

____

Can you think of a time when you were helpful to someone else and it reduced your stress or anger level, too? ______________________________

____

____

____

If being helpful to others can increase your peace, is there something you might be able to do today to help someone else? ______________________________

____

____

____

____

This art is a gift to GOGI from Haro

INCREASING MY PEACE – ACCOUNTABILITY BOX

DO YOU WANT CREDIT FOR THIS COURSE? REMEMBER TO KEEP TRACK OF YOUR DAILY STUDY BY COMPLETING THE INFORMATION BELOW TO GET YOUR CREDIT.

The month is________________; The day is ________________; The year is________; Solo study or group? ____________

Week 4

PLANNING YOUR REACTIONS CHAPTER

Have you read about these tools in this book yet? If not, you are cheating yourself of important information that will help you be the best version of you. Before you start with this week's study, please do yourself a favor and take a moment to read about these tools in this and other GOGI books. Then, continue with today's study.

Day 1 – YOU ARE THE BOSS

It may seem impossible to believe but your reactions are your choice. No one FORCES you to react in a particular way. You may "feel" as if you have no choice, or that they are pushing your buttons to "force" you to react a specific way, but the truth of the matter is that you have a choice in how you will react.

For individuals caught up in politics that dictate actions and behaviors it may seem as if you are trapped into reacting as you are told. And, in truth, you may have very limited choices, but you still have choices. You can choose what to read. You can choose what to say. You can choose what to think. You can choose how you feel. You can choose what goes on between your ears inside that powerful brain that only you can control.

When you read that you are the boss, even if you are limited in your ability to make your own decisions, how might this help you increase the level of peace you feel in your daily life? __________

____

If I am the boss, then... ____

____

____

If you know someone who feels trapped in a situation that controls much of their decision-making, how does this alter your perspective of what this individual might be experiencing? __________

____

____

____

*When I see people who feel trapped, I think...*______________________________

____

____

____

INCREASING MY PEACE – ACCOUNTABILITY BOX

DO YOU WANT CREDIT FOR THIS COURSE? REMEMBER TO KEEP TRACK OF YOUR DAILY STUDY BY COMPLETING THE INFORMATION BELOW TO GET YOUR CREDIT.

The month is____________________; The day is ____________________; The year is____________; Solo study or group? ________________

Day 1 – YOU ARE THE BOSS (continued)

Preparing to have a peaceful life requires you to choose peaceful reactions to situations that might normally stir up your anger. How might BOSS OF MY BRAIN help you with your choice of reactions?

Did you know that sometimes a person's family members and friends actually "miss" a person's anger and outrage and outbursts? That is right. Sometimes families and friends are suffering from dysfunction and depression and addiction and just about everything else. When YOU get angry, you take the attention off of their pain and struggles. You become the person to point fingers at as the problem. Sometimes, friends and family poke and poke trying to get the "old" you back.

What do you think about well-meaning family and friends actually "missing" the angry version of you and trying to get that part of you back? Is that messed up? How would you deal with that situation?

____

____

____

In your opinion, what is the most difficult part of change? ____________________

____

____

Is change easier when family and friends are encouraging? Why? ____________________

____

____

____

How difficult do you think it would be to remain on a solid path when everyone around you is messing up? ____________________

____

____

____

What can you do to protect your progress? ____________________

____

____

____

____

INCREASING MY PEACE – ACCOUNTABILITY BOX

DO YOU WANT CREDIT FOR THIS COURSE? REMEMBER TO KEEP TRACK OF YOUR DAILY STUDY BY COMPLETING THE INFORMATION BELOW TO GET YOUR CREDIT.

The month is________________; The day is ______________; The year is________; Solo study or group? ____________

LIFE HAPPENS

Your story:

We ALL do things and say things we later regret. On this page, please write about one time when you lost your temper and came to regret it:

The reason I got angry was because: ______________________________

____

____

____

____

There were things that led up to that time, things that had me not thinking clearly enough to make positive decisions. Some of these things were: ______________________________

____

____

____

____

Do you think that under different circumstances you might have reacted differently to a similar situation? How and why? ______________________________

____

____

____

____

Now write about that situation again but this time imagine using BOSS OF MY BRAIN and write a different outcome to that situation. What would have been different if you had used your GOGI Tools? ______________________________

____

____

____

____

____

INCREASING MY PEACE – ACCOUNTABILITY BOX

DO YOU WANT CREDIT FOR THIS COURSE? REMEMBER TO KEEP TRACK OF YOUR DAILY STUDY BY COMPLETING THE INFORMATION BELOW TO GET YOUR CREDIT.

The month is________________; The day is ________________; The year is__________; Solo study or group? ____________

Day 2 – YOU CAN USE BELLY BREATHING

Your body reacts in a more powerful and productive manner when you are breathing properly. You will give the impression that you are more powerful and less erratic when you use BELLY BREATHING. You will give the impression of being more in control, wiser, smarter, more mature, and more stable when you use BELLY BREATHING. Why? When you do not take full and relaxed breaths, your decisions and your reactions may be ones you later regret.

Think of it like this. BELLY BREATHING gives you time to plan your reactions. Without BELLY BREATHING you may be inclined toward "panic" breathing or a "fight or flight" mentality brought on by lack of oxygen to your body. This is a "survival" type of function your body resorts to when it seems there are no other options. When you are panic breathing and reacting, you are limited in your options of reactions. You are choosing reactions based on fear. With planned reactions to likely scenarios, you are more likely to get the outcome you want. Planned reactions require BELLY BREATHING.

The more you practice BELLY BREATHING the more likely you are to use this type of breathing even in the most challenging of circumstances.

What could you do today to help train your body to get enough oxygen so that you are making more positive decisions? ____

____

____

Would it help to pray? Meditate? Read? Walk the yard? Write a letter? Help someone else? Write down some things you might do to get more oxygen into your body. ____________________________

____

____

What are the things you could do today to begin to train your body to use BELLY BREATHING as the only way to breathe? What might you do to practice and master BELLY BREATHING?

I could:

1) ____

2) ____

3) ____

4) ____

5) ____

*What are the keywords for BELLY BREATHING?*____________________________

____

INCREASING MY PEACE – ACCOUNTABILITY BOX

DO YOU WANT CREDIT FOR THIS COURSE? REMEMBER TO KEEP TRACK OF YOUR DAILY STUDY BY COMPLETING THE INFORMATION BELOW TO GET YOUR CREDIT.

The month is________________; The day is ______________; The year is________; Solo study or group? ____________

FOLLOWING THE LEADER

Humans have a tendency to copy other humans. If someone is angry, then others are likely to become angry. If someone is BELLY BREATHING it is likely that others may begin to breathe more fully. Most humans will react and respond to others, permitting others to dictate their actions and reactions. And, truthfully, it might just be easier to go along with the crowd so you don't get singled out and struggle with the fallout of wanting to improve your life.

The good thing about the GOGI Tools is that you can use most of them without disrupting too many people. This is because most of the GOGI Tools can be done in silence and autonomy. Take BELLY BREATHING for example. While the entire yard can be operating on fear-based, panic breathing, you can remain alert and aware to dangers and still use BELLY BREATHING to get oxygen to your entire body. In this way, you are breaking free from the limitations of "prison yard" thinking by getting more oxygen in your body so you can steer clear of danger that might be lurking around the corner. You can master the fine art of BELLY BREATHING without anyone ever realizing that you are changing – from the inside out.

In your opinion, to what extent is the "attitude" of individuals in prison dictated by negative expectations or the negative "culture" that has existed for generations? ____________________

____

____

____

To what extent could you see using BELLY BREATHING to carve yourself a space to get out of that mentality? ____

____

____

____

As the prison system continues to evolve and offer more opportunities for prisoners to develop their ability to create a successful life, what are parts of your life you know are important for you to improve? ____

I want to improve in the following areas: ____________________________

1) ____

2) ____

3) ____

4) ____

5) ____

INCREASING MY PEACE – ACCOUNTABILITY BOX

DO YOU WANT CREDIT FOR THIS COURSE? REMEMBER TO KEEP TRACK OF YOUR DAILY STUDY BY COMPLETING THE INFORMATION BELOW TO GET YOUR CREDIT.

The month is________________; The day is ______________; The year is________; Solo study or group? __________

LIFE HAPPENS

Your Story:

As you look back on your life, would you say that shallow breathing might have contributed to some of the poor decisions you made? Why? ______________________________

____

____

Can you be specific about one particular time when fear, anger, or anxiety took hold and your actions followed? ______________________________

____

How old were you? ______________________________

Where were you? ______________________________

When you think about your past as a young child, were you aware of your breathing? Or did you assume that how you were breathing was natural? ______________________________

____

____

*Write about one time as a very young person when shallow or fearful breathing or anger (which shortens the breath) may have played a part in your poor decisions.*______________________________

____

If you had been taught GOGI Tools, what is an alternative reaction your might have had? ________

____

____

____

*As you think back, how many of your poor decisions might have been different had you used your GOGI Tools?*______________________________

____

____

How might your relationship be different with BELLY BREATHING? ______________________________

____

____

INCREASING MY PEACE – ACCOUNTABILITY BOX

DO YOU WANT CREDIT FOR THIS COURSE? REMEMBER TO KEEP TRACK OF YOUR DAILY STUDY BY COMPLETING THE INFORMATION BELOW TO GET YOUR CREDIT.

The month is________________; The day is ______________; The year is________; Solo study or group? ____________

Day 3 – YOU CAN FLIP YOUR SWITCH

Using FIVE SECOND LIGHTSWITCH to alter the course of events is probably one of the simplest things you can do to establish power over your life. When your mind begins to drift off a successful course, you can FLIP THAT SWITCH and instantly do something positive. By doing something positive, your mind must pay attention to what you are doing and it will LET GO of the thoughts that could have led you down a bad road.

FIVE SECOND LIGHTSWITCH is a diversion tactic used by skilled parents, astute teachers, and solid leaders. It is easy to divert thoughts into POSITIVE ACTIONS. It is much more difficult to try to stop the negative thought. It's kind of like a bait and switch technique. Your mind may want a drink of alcohol but you can FLIP THE SWITCH and give it something else to do, like 200 sit-ups and long drink of water.

You are retraining your brain to self-correct, and pick something positive rather than those things you are changing in your life.

How might you explain FIVE SECOND LIGHTSWITCH to an impulsive youngster who just got to prison at the start of a 25 year sentence? What would you tell him – IF he WERE willing to listen? _

I know that you... ____

____

____

____

____

The important aspect of FIVE SECOND LIGHTSWITCH is to have preplanned POSITIVE ACTIONS ready to replace a negative thought. It is OK to try to change the thought to a POSITIVE THOUGHT but it is far more powerful if you swap the negative thought with a POSITIVE ACTION. This act of getting to an action engages the entire body, not just the thinking process. If the entire body is engaged in something positive then you have a better chance of eliminating the annoyance of the negative thought.

If you knew that simply doing something positive within five seconds of a negative thought was as powerful as GOGI students claim, would you share this concept with others? If so, who do you think might benefit the most from understanding this concept? ______________________

____

____

How would you suggest they apply this to their lives? ______________________

____

____

INCREASING MY PEACE – ACCOUNTABILITY BOX

DO YOU WANT CREDIT FOR THIS COURSE? REMEMBER TO KEEP TRACK OF YOUR DAILY STUDY BY COMPLETING THE INFORMATION BELOW TO GET YOUR CREDIT.

The month is________________; The day is ______________; The year is________; Solo study or group? __________

LIFE HAPPENS

Your Story:

Let's say you are able to go back in time to your teens or those critical years where you started to make poor choices. Let's say that you are at the year when critical choices are being made about the grownup you will become. Let's also say that there is no one around who you respect enough to listen to when they tell you that you are headed down a bad path. If there was any way that you could have used FIVE SECOND LIGHTSWITCH how could you have used this tool? Let's say that you slowed down enough to realize that you were headed down a path of destruction. What FIVE SECOND LIGHTSWITCH might you have flipped to begin to alter the direction of your life?

Now let's say that a new guy comes on to the yard and he reminds you of yourself. You see the look in his eye and the way he holds himself. You can pretty much guess what is going on in his mind. He approaches you to ask you if you know so-and-so and you take the opportunity to take this youngster under your wing and help him out. He is nearly begging for you to help him get home and stay home. What would you tell him about your own youth and his future?

*This is how I thought when I was a kid...*______________________________

____

____

____

These are some of the freedoms I lost because of my thinking and actions... ______________

____

____

This is what I need to do to get more freedom... __________________________

____

____

____

____

*This is what I hope for you and your life...*____________________________

____

____

____

____

INCREASING MY PEACE – ACCOUNTABILITY BOX

DO YOU WANT CREDIT FOR THIS COURSE? REMEMBER TO KEEP TRACK OF YOUR DAILY STUDY BY COMPLETING THE INFORMATION BELOW TO GET YOUR CREDIT.

The month is________________; The day is ________________; The year is________; Solo study or group? ____________

Day 4 – TOOLS OF THE BODY

The GOGI TOOLS OF THE BODY are tools designed by prisoners, of course. They were also created at different times by different prisoners. And, they did not label the section of tools called TOOLS OF THE BODY until many years after they were gifted to GOGI. The TOOLS OF THE BODY permit you to create, generate, maintain, support, and sustain control and command over your body's reaction to life's inevitable challenges.

This control that you can develop will permit a huge increase in your level of internal peace. When you KNOW beyond any doubt that you have BOSS OF MY BRAIN, BELLY BREATHING, and FIVE SECOND LIGHTSWITCH to command control of your body, then no one is able to control you or push your buttons. You will never say, "he made me do it," or other weak responses to losing your temper or reacting poorly.

With the TOOLS OF THE BODY you are, ultimately, in control. Some GOGI students state that these three tools freed them from a prison they felt would always remain, even after they were released from prison.

Why do you think some people struggle with an internal prison created by lack of command over their own body and mind? ______________________________

____

____

Why do you think the TOOLS OF THE BODY seem to be so simple for these individuals to understand and apply to their lives? ______________________________

____

____

It's pretty common knowledge that some Corrections Officers experience prisoners as erratic, demanding, unreasonable, and short-fused. Similarly, some Corrections Officers find other prisoners are peaceful, educated, mindful, and respectful of authority. If there are two "types" of prisoners in the mind of some Corrections Officers, which type of prisoner do you think would be the type to have command over the GOGI Tools? Which type would be the best neighbor upon release? Which type would be the best on the job, or in a relationship, or alone with their thoughts?

*Could you see the GOGI TOOLS OF THE BODY as a set of tools to be taught to all prisoners? What about all school children, long before they start acting out their frustrations?*________________

____

____

____

____

INCREASING MY PEACE – ACCOUNTABILITY BOX

DO YOU WANT CREDIT FOR THIS COURSE? REMEMBER TO KEEP TRACK OF YOUR DAILY STUDY BY COMPLETING THE INFORMATION BELOW TO GET YOUR CREDIT.

The month is__________________; The day is ________________; The year is________; Solo study or group? __________

LIFE HAPPENS

Your Life:

Let's say you volunteer to speak to a youth group that will be touring the prison. Your topic is FLIPPING THE SWITCH. You need to get this tool into the hearts of these students so they can handle the challenges and decisions they are facing as they create their life with their choices in their teens.

Use this space to write your two-minute talk on THE POWER OF FLIPPING THE SWITCH. First, let me tell you a little about me. I was the kind of kid: ______________________________

____

____

____

I used to believe that: ____

____

____

____

This belief led to my: ____

____

____

____

____

I am going to give you some wisdom: listen up. Flipping the switch means you can: __________

____

____

____

____

____

____

____

____

INCREASING MY PEACE – ACCOUNTABILITY BOX

DO YOU WANT CREDIT FOR THIS COURSE? REMEMBER TO KEEP TRACK OF YOUR DAILY STUDY BY COMPLETING THE INFORMATION BELOW TO GET YOUR CREDIT.

The month is________________; The day is ______________; The year is________; Solo study or group? ____________

Day 5 - YOUR TOOL BOX

GOGI students study their tools according to the calendar, but in this course only the first three weeks were studied according to the calendar. The balance of the course was reinforcing what tools you used. But, the idea is that you not stop your study of GOGI when this course is over. The idea is that you jump right back into your study of your GOGI Tools according to the calendar and you will have a strong knowledge of the TOOLS OF THE BODY.

In this course you are engaged in intense study of one section of tools. For two full months you are reading and writing and engaging in reflective thought, as well as considering use of these tools in the future. This level of engagement is needed for success and mastery. While some students claim that the repetition is "boring" it is only with repetition that mastery is attained.

When you read that this course is an intense study of one section of tools and that the repetition is necessary for mastery of the tool, what thoughts come to your mind? What challenges does repetition pose? And what are the risks of NOT repeating something over and over again? ______________

____

____

____

MASTERY OF ANYTHING

To become a skilled thief a person had to take something that was not theirs and then repeat that process over and over again. To be an alcoholic, the person needed to take that first drink and then suck on the end of the bottle again and again and again. To become known for beating women, the man needed to hit a girl or woman for the first time, and continue to abuse over and over. This building of negative skills is the exact process used to build a positive skill. The problem is that once we have a skill, we identify with it as if it is a part of who we are. Actually, it is just a habit we have developed. And, at any time, we can develop a positive habit.

Good readers are not born, they just are people who practice reading long enough to be good at it. Good fathers and mothers are not born, they are just individuals who are mindful of how they behave in the role of parent. Good GOGI Coaches are not born, they are just individuals who have practiced their GOGI Tools for so long that the tools become part of how they define themselves.

When you think of mastery of any skill, are there some positive skills that you would like to master? Some qualities you would like to develop so you can increase your peace? If it took many years to develop negative skills, are you prepared to hang in there and develop positive skills over a sustained period of time as well? ____

____

____

____

____

INCREASING MY PEACE – ACCOUNTABILITY BOX

DO YOU WANT CREDIT FOR THIS COURSE? REMEMBER TO KEEP TRACK OF YOUR DAILY STUDY BY COMPLETING THE INFORMATION BELOW TO GET YOUR CREDIT.

The month is____________; The day is ____________; The year is________; Solo study or group? ________

LIFE HAPPENS

Your Life:

There is likely to be a long list of skills and talents you have developed that you don't really pay much attention to or acknowledge. These are likely to be things you repeated over and over again until you became good at them. For some, it may be a skill of making and keeping lifelong friends. For others, it may be the ability to listen to children in a way that makes them feel understood. For others it may be the skill of fixing a car, or drawing a beautiful picture. For others it may be the skill of religious understandings, or the skill of seeing the best in everyone.

Below please write the many good skills you have developed in your lifetime, those things that people have commented on or things that make you feel good inside when you can contribute to others. What are your skills and how did you develop them?

*People say I am good at:*________________________________

____

____

____

*I really enjoy doing the following things:*________________________

____

____

I can make life better for others when I: ________________________

____

____

*When looking at your skills, can you imagine picking one GOGI Tool and adding mastery of that Tool to your skill list? If you picked mastery of any of the GOGI Tools, which one would it be and how might your mastery of this tool benefit you and all those who are around you?*______________

____

____

____

*How long do you think it would take to truly master this tool and use it without thinking, as a new habit and new way of being?*________________________

____

____

____

INCREASING MY PEACE – ACCOUNTABILITY BOX

DO YOU WANT CREDIT FOR THIS COURSE? REMEMBER TO KEEP TRACK OF YOUR DAILY STUDY BY COMPLETING THE INFORMATION BELOW TO GET YOUR CREDIT.

The month is________________; The day is ______________; The year is________; Solo study or group? ____________

Day 6 – MASTERY TAKES TIME

The challenge in the process of change is the fact that it takes repetition over a sustained period of time. Prisoners become "institutionalized" if they repeat the prison mentality over and over again, year after year. Prisoners can also identify their internal freedom if they practice those things that are self-corrective and enhancing to the human experience. The choice is yours. You will repeat SOMETHING in your life and it will either be negative or positive, based on your choices. You will either become institutionalized to a negative culture or you will make the difficult decision to turn away from what is easy and really dive into your own mind and body and soul and begin the reconstruction project from the inside out – building new skills over a sustained period of time.

For those who choose to go along with the crowd, there is anger, discontent, isolation, violence, fear, intimidation, and lack of internal freedom. For those who focus on those things which are possibly less popular, they must sustain this commitment to inner freedom under massive pushback from friends and sometimes family.

When you read the above, what does this make you think? How does the "institutionalized" mentality keep prisoners in prison? What needs to happen in your own life so you can be an example of increasing your peace and ultimately finding your freedom – even while locked up? ____________

If there are 900 prisoners on a yard, how many of them would need to be GOGI Coaches before the culture on that yard would be positive and prepare all prisoners to return to society as productive citizens? ____________

Of the 900 prisoners, how many do you believe would actually WANT a positive culture on the yard? How many would resist the change but ultimately see the benefit to their families and loved ones?

A shift in culture is happening in prisons. Do you see yourself as being part of the solution or is the problem too big right now? ____________

INCREASING MY PEACE – ACCOUNTABILITY BOX

DO YOU WANT CREDIT FOR THIS COURSE? REMEMBER TO KEEP TRACK OF YOUR DAILY STUDY BY COMPLETING THE INFORMATION BELOW TO GET YOUR CREDIT.

The month is________________; The day is ______________; The year is________; Solo study or group? ____________

Day 7 – Recap and Review

What are the three tools in the section called TOOLS OF THE BODY? (Hint: The three tools you have learned so far in this course)

1) ____

2) ____

3) ____

Of the three tools you have learned so far in this course, which one do you feel might be most effective in your life? Why do you think this? ____

____

____

____

In this course you are actually planning your reactions to life's inevitable challenges. Do you think by planning your reactions you will have a better chance at reacting in a way that helps you move forward in your life? Why or why not? How are you a better person when you apply your GOGI Tools? ____

____

____

What are some specific ways you can remember your tools? ____

____

____

*When you are rattled, how can you flip the switch?*____

____

____

____

Complete this sentence: I want people to see that I am... ____

____

____

____

____

GOGI train a gift to GOGI from Rey

GOGI

A short nuemonic story to help us remember the names and order of our GOGI tools.

I woke up this morning as the BOSS OF MY BRAIN while BELLY BREATHING and searching for the FIVE SECOND LIGHTSWITCH. My mind was filled with POSITIVE THOUGHTS, POSITIVE WORDS, and POSITIVE ACTIONS. As I CLAIM RESPONSIBILITY I LET GO of my problems FOR me to GIVE. I ask myself, "WHAT IF I am not my past?" Do I need a REALITY CHECK so I can achieve ULTIMATE FREEDOM.

Jason R. Boman

CCI, Tehachapi

Simple tools for Life's many challenges.

DO YOU WANT CREDIT FOR THIS COURSE? REMEMBER TO KEEP TRACK OF YOUR DAILY STUDY BY COMPLETING THE INFORMATION BELOW TO GET YOUR CREDIT.

The month is________________; The day is ______________; The year is________; Solo study or group? ____________

YOUR STRATEGY PAGE

This page is provided for you to answer questions you may eventually be asked about strategies you have for your future. You can start to formalize a plan so that when life serves up its inevitable challenges, you are prepared to handle them by INCREASING YOUR PEACE.

Humans are always more successful when they practice and plan how to handle things. When humans are unprepared or have not practiced, they are often less successful than those who DO practice and plan. This is your page to write down a particular scenario you believe you may face in the future. Write this scenario down and then write about your plan to overcome all obstacles using your tools and your thoughtful planning.

This strategy could be related to a job, a relationship, a C.O., a move, a release, a denial of release, a death in the family, or even a smelly cellie. You build your plan on exactly how you can INCREASE THE PEACE in that situation.

Let's say your date for release is calculated wrong. You won't be released for another 146 days. You are more than mad. What do you do? How do you feel? ______________________________

____

____

Which friend do you reach out to first? ______________________________

____

Which tool comes to mind first? ______________________________

____

Let's say the people who promised to help you are suddenly not available when it comes time to step up to the plate and help you get home. What do you do? How do you feel? ______________

____

Which tool comes in most handy? ______________________________

____

Let's say work is not nearly as easy nor as pleasurable as you would have hoped. You really want to quit, but you need to pay family back for the money they have given you to get settled. You feel you won't ever get ahead. What do you do? ______________________________

____

Which tool can you use? ______________________________

____

____

INCREASING MY PEACE – ACCOUNTABILITY BOX

DO YOU WANT CREDIT FOR THIS COURSE? REMEMBER TO KEEP TRACK OF YOUR DAILY STUDY BY COMPLETING THE INFORMATION BELOW TO GET YOUR CREDIT.

The month is________________; The day is ______________; The year is________; Solo study or group? ____________

DEEP DIVING - Getting to the bottom of it

Here are two pages for you. On these pages, we want to know about your journey with your own anger. We want to know what caused your anger and how you are working towards increasing your peace. Refer to what you have studied this week and know that each week you will be permitted to jot down your thoughts and experiences related to your past, your present, and your future.

Thinking about this past week, do you think you have noticed things about people's reactions? Have you witnessed anger? If so, did you observe how the individual managed that anger?

____

____

*Does observing others strengthen or weaken you? Why?*____________________

____

____

In thinking about this past week, was there any time when you noticed your own thinking and you made a new type of decision about how to handle a situation? What was the situation?

____

____

____

How did it feel to make a different decision? ____________________

____

____

____

Remembering the last time you saw someone "lose it" over something they don't like, did your respect for that person increase or decrease with their outburst? And why do you think that is the case? __

____

____

____

*How might you earn more respect by using GOGI Tools?*____________________

____

____

____

DO YOU WANT CREDIT FOR THIS COURSE? REMEMBER TO KEEP TRACK OF YOUR DAILY STUDY BY COMPLETING THE INFORMATION BELOW TO GET YOUR CREDIT.

The month is________________; The day is ______________; The year is________; Solo study or group? __________

DEEP DIVING

Use these pages to write down how you might describe your own rehabilitation, or how to explain to a loved one how you are no longer the person you once were. However you use these pages, let them reflect your insight, your understanding, and your ability to be the best person you can be – today!

If someone asked you "are you going to be a good neighbor when you are released?" what would you say? List three ways in which you will be good neighbor. I will...

1) ______________________________

2) ______________________________

3) ______________________________

If someone were to look into your C-file and ask about the internal work you have done to become a better person, what might you share with them? ______________________________

Well, first I worked on: ______________________________

____

Then I: ______________________________

____

Finally I: ______________________________

____

Now I: ______________________________

____

When you are sitting in your first job interview and the guy asks if you have ever been to prison? How can you describe to him your past, but also the skills and dedication you bring to any job you might be given? ______________________________

____

____

____

How can your past be shared without any shame or embarrassment? ______________________________

____

____

____

BELLY BREATHING
BOSS OF MY BRAIN
FIVE SECOND LIGHT SWITCH
POSITIVE
CLAIM RESPONSIBILITY
LET GO
FORGIVE
WHAT IF
Thoughts
ACTIONS 2 GROW
REALITY CHECK
ULTIMATE FREEDOM
AnthonyLewi

INCREASING MY PEACE – ACCOUNTABILITY BOX

DO YOU WANT CREDIT FOR THIS COURSE? REMEMBER TO KEEP TRACK OF YOUR DAILY STUDY BY COMPLETING THE INFORMATION BELOW TO GET YOUR CREDIT.

The month is________________; The day is ______________; The year is________; Solo study or group? ____________

Week 5

PLANNING YOUR FUTURE USING TOOLS OF THE BODY

DAY 1 — YOUR CHOICE

You may not have many choices in your life but the one choice no one can take from you is your choice to respond and react as you want. You can respond and react to anything in life in a manner that increases your internal peace. Or you can respond and react in a manner that disrupts your internal peace and makes you angry.

You can be told to stand in a line or up against a wall and unless you want to be written up, you will follow those instructions. But no one can control how you respond or react to standing against the wall. Similarly, you may not be able to control where you live when you are released, or what job you are offered but HOW you respond and react to things beyond your control is completely and totally within your control.

You have the power to choose how you will react, and your level of peace is related to your choice. To say, "they made me do it," or "I had no choice but to hit him," or "what do you expect? Look what they did!" are all weak responses that diminish your power to secure a sense of peace in your life.

Given what you have learned so far in this course, how might using the GOGI Tools help you better manage your responses and reactions when you are being treated in a manner you believe you do not deserve? ____

____

With BOSS OF MY BRAIN I now know... ____

____

____

With BELLY BREATHING I can now... ____

____

____

With FIVE SECOND LIGHTSWITCH I can... ____

____

____

These tools help me to realize... ____

____

INCREASING MY PEACE – ACCOUNTABILITY BOX

DO YOU WANT CREDIT FOR THIS COURSE? REMEMBER TO KEEP TRACK OF YOUR DAILY STUDY BY COMPLETING THE INFORMATION BELOW TO GET YOUR CREDIT.

The month is________________; The day is ________________; The year is__________; Solo study or group? ____________

Day 1 – LIFE IS NOT FAIR

Life is not often fair, but it is frequently and predictably unfair. Nice people do not inherently receive better treatment or more opportunities than jerks or mean people. Mean and angry people sometimes run over nice people and grab things that are not necessarily earned. Some people lie. They cheat. They steal. And, funny enough, the people who are caught in the cycle of trying to exact their own level of "fairness" through unfair means are oftentimes suffering from depression or addictions as a result of their distorted perspective on life's "fairness."

When we understand that life is not a balanced scale but we can balance our own internal scale, then we begin to experience increased internal peace. When we develop the ability to create increased internal peace then more peaceful things surround us. When more peaceful things surround us, we begin to experience the world as a bit more "fair."

1) When you read the paragraphs above, what do you think? Did you once suffer from a focus on what was "fair" and how you were in some way cheated in the big balancing scales of life? ______

2) And/or how does this perspective on things resonate with your own life experiences and observations? ______

3) How can you apply any of this to your future and your desire for a peaceful life? ______

INCREASING MY PEACE – ACCOUNTABILITY BOX

DO YOU WANT CREDIT FOR THIS COURSE? REMEMBER TO KEEP TRACK OF YOUR DAILY STUDY BY COMPLETING THE INFORMATION BELOW TO GET YOUR CREDIT.

The month is______________; The day is ______________; The year is_________; Solo study or group? ______________

LIFE HAPPENS

Your Future.

Regardless of what you may now believe, it is likely that at some point in your life you will be released from prison and you will be physically "free." Remember, however, that there is a difference between physical freedom and internal freedom. Internal freedom is rarely experienced by anyone, in or out of prison.

What are your thoughts on this fact that internal freedom is a far more rare release? __________

____

____

____

____

*How can you maintain your internal freedom once you receive your physical freedom?*__________

____

____

____

____

*What is your plan for increasing your peace even after you are released from physical custody?*____

____

____

____

____

____

In your opinion what is the difference between physical freedom and internal freedom? ________

____

____

____

____

____

INCREASING MY PEACE – ACCOUNTABILITY BOX

DO YOU WANT CREDIT FOR THIS COURSE? REMEMBER TO KEEP TRACK OF YOUR DAILY STUDY BY COMPLETING THE INFORMATION BELOW TO GET YOUR CREDIT.

The month is________________; The day is ________________; The year is________; Solo study or group? ____________

Day 2 – OVERLY OPTIMISTIC

Most prisoners have dreams and expectations of the day they will be released. Oftentimes they have unrealistic expectations of what physical freedom means and they are unprepared for the challenges they face as they attempt to adjust to a new environment.

After their release, the formerly incarcerated individual is oftentimes disappointed with the struggle that begins the very moment they walk beyond the wall. This excessive optimism about physical freedom often leaves formerly incarcerated individuals angry and frustrated, as their dreams may seem impossible and they experience a different form of "prison" on the outside.

Being overly optimistic is a natural human trait and it can be balanced with a deep understanding of the skills and talents that are needed to maintain a sense of peace and freedom.

In this course you have studied tools to aid you in increasing your peace. Increasing your peace, however, has a lot to do with your expectations and your preparation to face and overcome challenges in the future.

After reading the information above, write your plan for dealing with unmet expectations, broken promises, and unforeseen disappointments in the future. ____________________________

____

____

____

____

SUCCESS – THE WINNERS AND THE LOSERS

When an individual has worked really hard to develop a sense of internal peace while incarcerated, they are oftentimes better equipped to manage life's challenges when they are released back into society. In their study and practice of self-help tools, and in their dedication to making positive decisions, they have practiced over and over again how to appropriately respond to challenges. It is in the repetition of things that we become skilled. Skill requires repeated practice.

*How is increasing your peace while you are incarcerated a way to have more success upon your release? How is diligent study during prison linked with success post release? How might the GOGI Tools assist in maintaining high levels of internal peace under any circumstance?*____________

____

____

____

____

____

DO YOU WANT CREDIT FOR THIS COURSE? REMEMBER TO KEEP TRACK OF YOUR DAILY STUDY BY COMPLETING THE INFORMATION BELOW TO GET YOUR CREDIT.

The month is________________; The day is ______________; The year is________; Solo study or group? _____________

LIFE HAPPENS

Let's say that two cellies are released on the same day. One man spent most of his time in classes, with chaplains, working on correspondence courses, attending workshops, and generally associating with positive and productive people. The other cellie only had five years to do so he did not see the point of signing up on a course list with a one-year waitlist. He chose to spend his five years making friends and talking and hanging out on the yard and networking with other guys doing their time the way he was doing his.

Fast forward to one year after they are released. What do you imagine the studious formerly incarcerated individual is doing with his days? And, if you had to guess, what do you think his cellie does each day? Who do you think has an easier time remaining law-abiding and far away from parole's heavy hand? Why do you think this is a fact? ____

____

____

____

*How is a person's behavior inside prison a good indicator of behavior when they are released?*_____

____

____

____

____

What do you think it would take to get every prisoner to understand that now is the time to increase their levels of peace through their choices in how they spend their time each day? ____________

____

____

____

____

How might you suggest to others that the investment in their future is well worth the sacrifices of hanging out with the neighborhood friends? ____

____

____

____

____

INCREASING MY PEACE – ACCOUNTABILITY BOX

DO YOU WANT CREDIT FOR THIS COURSE? REMEMBER TO KEEP TRACK OF YOUR DAILY STUDY BY COMPLETING THE INFORMATION BELOW TO GET YOUR CREDIT.

The month is________________; The day is _______________; The year is_________; Solo study or group? ____________

Day 3 – MASTERY OF YOUR TOOLS

In this course you have reviewed three tools of GOGI: BOSS OF MY BRAIN, BELLY BREATHING, and FIVE SECOND LIGHTSWITCH. These tools are powerful when used together, but they can be used individually as well. Individually or as part of your positive decision-making a tool kit, these TOOLS OF THE BODY can help you steer away from anger and help you make choices that lead to increasing your peace.

Even if you have been a student of GOGI for a long time, it is likely you are not yet an expert in the use of these tools. Similar to a car mechanic, you can't be expert at fixing cars the first time you get your hands on a wrench. It takes years to build a skill. Using your GOGI Tools and becoming a master craftsman will take time and dedication. Those who say that GOGI didn't work for them are invariably those who walked away just moments before their interest turned into a skill.

*When thinking about your ability to develop talents and skills, where in your life have you dedicated time, energy, thought, and persistence in achieving your goals? Can you see that any skill will take time and energy? Can you see that your skills can be taken with you when you are released and headed home? Have you walked away from something positive before? Why? And why is it now different for you?*____

____

____

ANGRY PEOPLE CRITICIZE OTHERS

Have you ever noticed that angry people are also those who spend an inordinate amount of time criticizing others? Angry people are drawn to criticism and will choose to cut people down instead of moving on to something less negative. It's as if their anger is a magnet to all the negativity around them, drawing in all the toxic people and activities which exacerbates their anger even more.

In fact, angry people will often pass right by something that is good and positive and intentionally seek out something to criticize. Furthermore, the anger can spread its toxic waste into otherwise neutral situations.

Using BOSS OF MY BRAIN, you can quickly move from the toxicity of anger to a more neutral experience, choosing to use the SMART PART of your brain. You can use BELLY BREATHING and get the oxygen throughout your body, which will help with your decision-making. And you can flip your FIVE SECOND LIGHTSWITCH and choose your POSITIVE ACTION to divert you from any possibility of a poor decision.

When reading the above, can you relate to the "energy" that angry people carry with them? Does this apply in your own life, or as you witness anger in others? How much could the GOGI Tools be helpful when the toxicity of anger begins to spread? ________________________________

____

____

INCREASING MY PEACE – ACCOUNTABILITY BOX

DO YOU WANT CREDIT FOR THIS COURSE? REMEMBER TO KEEP TRACK OF YOUR DAILY STUDY BY COMPLETING THE INFORMATION BELOW TO GET YOUR CREDIT.

The month is________________; The day is ______________; The year is________; Solo study or group? ____________

LIFE HAPPENS

RJ has been an angry man since before he was a man. He had trouble in school but that only came after trouble at home. It seems to RJ as if "angry" is just what he is, that it's part of his DNA and part of what makes him RJ. To not be angry is foreign to RJ. The only time he remembers not being angry is after a six-pack and a good smoke. RJ has even remained angry for 24 years of the life sentence he didn't think he deserved because he was defending himself from someone even more angry than he has ever been. In any case, a new law was passed that flagged him for a possible relook at the amount of time he should serve.

RJ is not prepared. He was too busy being angry at the world. He sees you preparing every day for your release in ways that he previously teased you about. Now, quite humbly for RJ, he is asking what steps he should take to make the changes the Board will want to see to give him his freedom.

"I never thought I had a chance of getting out of here," he says to you as you put your GOGI books down on your desk. "The thing is, I have wasted 24 years. Where do I begin?

Below, write out your strategy to help RJ catch up on all the self-help that he has missed in more than two decades.

Well, RJ," you say, "it's like this..." ____

____

____

Let me tell you a little about BOSS OF MY BRAIN... __________________________________

____

____

____

____

*Here's the scoop on BELLY BREATHING so you can...*___________________________________

____

____

____

*And, finally, you have FIVE SECOND LIGHTSWITCH which means...*______________________

____

____

____

INCREASING MY PEACE – ACCOUNTABILITY BOX

DO YOU WANT CREDIT FOR THIS COURSE? REMEMBER TO KEEP TRACK OF YOUR DAILY STUDY BY COMPLETING THE INFORMATION BELOW TO GET YOUR CREDIT.

The month is_______________; The day is _______________; The year is________; Solo study or group? ____________

Day 4 – ANTICIPATE AND PLAN

Your success in many - if not all - areas of your life is more likely when you can anticipate the possible negative and positive outcomes of any situation. When you strategically plan your actions and reactions to those possible scenarios, you are better equipped to respond positively. That is the beauty and the simplicity of the GOGI Tools. They let you have a simple tool for every possible situation just standing by and waiting to be used.

Some people say that you need to remain positive, and not plan for the worst, but there may be great wisdom in remaining positive and having a plan in place that you can activate if things do not turn out as planned. You don't need to sit around fearing the worst, but to plan adequately for difficulty and struggle permits you to be mature instead of wishful thinking.

What is your belief about being prepared for negative and positive outcomes? Do you see any value in planning how you will respond, even if an outcome is unlikely? How might you remain positive and still have a plan for how to handle something negative?

Your GOGI Tools will come in handy as you create your "B" plan, just in case your "A" plan for things falls through. In fact, it is quite likely that if you had used GOGI Tools, you would not have the ID number and the mailing address you currently have. Your skill at predicting possible outcomes and using your GOGI Tools could help you avoid a prison term or addiction or any other undesirable state. Not only does planning your responses to things help with remaining peaceful, amazing as it may seem, planning for different types of outcomes may help you maintain your cool when the "unexpected" happens.

1) While you cannot change the past, you can direct your future so the same mistakes are not made. How can you best plan for situations that increase your struggle or seem to be unfair or unjust?

____

____

____

2) How can a 'B' plan help you from getting angry? ____________________

____

____

____

3) How can you keep your peace intact as you move beyond the situation? ____________

____

____

____

____

DO YOU WANT CREDIT FOR THIS COURSE? REMEMBER TO KEEP TRACK OF YOUR DAILY STUDY BY COMPLETING THE INFORMATION BELOW TO GET YOUR CREDIT.

The month is________________; The day is ______________; The year is________; Solo study or group? _____________

LIFE HAPPENS

Your Life:

In your own life, do you believe that anger played a part in the decisions you've made? And, if so, were the decisions you made during a state of anger, decisions you later regretted?

If anger has not played a part in your decision-making process, how did you keep them separated?

____

____

____

Do you think you were instinctively using a form of the GOGI Tools? ____________________

____

____

____

As you look at how you have grown and changed over the years, do you think some aspects of your anger have managed to improve? ______________________________

____

____

____

How might accomplishing this course strengthen your ability to continue your growth? ________

____

____

____

____

Write thoughts that are on your mind about your future growth, and your ability to increase your peace. ______________________________________

____

____

____

____

____

INCREASING MY PEACE – ACCOUNTABILITY BOX

DO YOU WANT CREDIT FOR THIS COURSE? REMEMBER TO KEEP TRACK OF YOUR DAILY STUDY BY COMPLETING THE INFORMATION BELOW TO GET YOUR CREDIT.

The month is________________; The day is ______________; The year is________; Solo study or group? __________

Day 5 - THE UNEXPECTED ANGER

There is a fine line between being negative and being aware of possible negative situations. The mastery comes when you can perceive possibilities and not get too rattled by them. One person might say, "I am not going to schedule a visit because this yard goes down every other weekend," and the other person might warn the potential visitor "Hey, I want you to come, but where I am gets locked down a lot. I want you to make sure you call before you put gas in your tank and head all the way up here."

Given the two different possible reactions, which person is likely to have an increased level of peace and which one might struggle with buried anger? Why do you believe this? ____________

____

____

____

How is your "attitude" toward a situation a determining factor in your response when bad things happen? Or, in your own life, how has your ability to see possible negative outcomes protected you from unwanted anger and increased your peace? ____________________

____

____

____

If you were to sit down with both of the individuals above after the yard got off lockdown, how would you speak to them about how YOU manage to plan for the worst but remain open for the best possible outcome? ____________________________________

____

____

____

____

How can your GOGI Tools help you in situations like these, where things beyond your control can really mess up your plans? ____________________________

____

____

____

____

____

DO YOU WANT CREDIT FOR THIS COURSE? REMEMBER TO KEEP TRACK OF YOUR DAILY STUDY BY COMPLETING THE INFORMATION BELOW TO GET YOUR CREDIT.

The month is________________; The day is ______________; The year is________; Solo study or group? ____________

LIFE HAPPENS

Let's say you manage to get to a housing unit where the C.O.s are surprisingly supportive of having the prisoners study and read together. While it is not in their requirements, most of the C.O.s will let you out of your cell and will let you go door-to-door and check in with the guys who are now doing IN-CELL GOGI STUDIES on their own. You are worried about JaRome, who just heard that his kid brother was killed by a rival gang. Somehow, the cops got word of this and now, somehow and for some reason, JaRome is getting yanked from this yard and placed in protective custody. You ask the C.O. if you can go to JaRome's door just to give him some words of encouragement. Since you have proven to be trouble-free for more than ten years, the C.O. pops open your door after everyone gets back from yard. You approach JaRome's window and you can see he has been crying.

What do you say? *Hey, man...Listen...Let me share something with you...*____________________

____

____

____

____

____

____

The C.O. gives you a few moments but then asks that you come to the desk where she and her partner are sitting.

"I have Officer Vasquez here and he is new to this yard. I was telling him that this block is no joke; these men want to go home and are really serious about changing. Tell him about GOGI," she says.

You know this is the beginning of a lifelong need to explain what GOGI is and how the tools help people, even officers, make better decisions.

What do you say? *Nice to meet you, Officer Vasquez. Well, in this block we almost all study GOGI. GOGI is...*

____

____

____

____

____

____

____

INCREASING MY PEACE – ACCOUNTABILITY BOX

DO YOU WANT CREDIT FOR THIS COURSE? REMEMBER TO KEEP TRACK OF YOUR DAILY STUDY BY COMPLETING THE INFORMATION BELOW TO GET YOUR CREDIT.

The month is________________; The day is ______________; The year is_________; Solo study or group? ____________

Day 6 – KICKED WHEN YOU ARE DOWN

There is a saying that sometimes life kicks you the hardest when you are down. Many people feel like bad things happen, and they can be managed, but then an entirely new wave of bad things topple in on those and it becomes insurmountable. Most relapses, whether in drugs or illegal actions, happen when the person has managed a great deal of adversity but then one thing happens that tips the scales and it seems too much to handle. The towel gets tossed and another rodeo ride begins.

For the majority of people who relapse into old behaviors, they can identify the incident that pushed them over the edge. It was usually the second or third wave of problems and the weight was just too much to overcome. Write down how the GOGI Tools could be helpful when the waves of problems keep hitting like a bad storm hitting the Florida shores.

*Even if you are not an addict to drugs or drinking, you may be addicted to anger or depression or just about anything else. Why might this be a fact?*________________________________

____

____

____

Remaining focused on the progress is key in overcoming storm after storm in your life. Consider some of the bad things that might happen to you in the future when you are returned to society (even if you are LWOP you must plan as laws change and people change and prepared people often get breaks that the unprepared do not). How can your tools keep you focused? ________________

____

____

____

____

____

*When the worst of the worst happens (which often happens) how will you manage your anger and increase your peace? Be specific. What MIGHT rattle your cage and shake your foundation? What tool do you have to help?*____

____

____

____

____

____

____

INCREASING MY PEACE – ACCOUNTABILITY BOX

DO YOU WANT CREDIT FOR THIS COURSE? REMEMBER TO KEEP TRACK OF YOUR DAILY STUDY BY COMPLETING THE INFORMATION BELOW TO GET YOUR CREDIT.

The month is________________; The day is ______________; The year is________; Solo study or group? ____________

LIFE HAPPENS

A guy named Ricky Martin is moved into your block. He likes being called Rico, but someone from his childhood is in the block and starts to tease him and telling him to "sing a song, Ricky Martin." You know the new kid is not a bad kid and you can tell he has been battered around because of his unfortunate resemblance to the singer Ricky Martin. You also see a group of old-school prisoners trying to include this youngster into their little "family" which undoubtedly would suck him into old-school prison politics. For his own protection, Rico seems as if he is headed that way, even though you know he does not truly have a criminal or gang mentality.

What do you do and why? ____

____

Is there a risk in helping those who are in need? ____

____

What are the risks you face when you help guide others to making positive decisions and not negative ones? ____

____

____

How can your decisions help change the culture from old-school prison politics to a culture that develops and supports future leaders and volunteers in communities that suffer? ____________

____

____

____

Rico thanks you for telling him about his options with different programming. He also tells you that his girlfriend is pregnant and he is not sure how he is going to handle the next seven years. What makes him most angry is that once he was sentenced, his former best friend started showing up to "help" his girl. Now, not even two years into his time, his girl is not writing any more.

What is the first GOGI Tool you share with Rico and why? Why did you choose the tool you chose? Maybe you even permit him to take a look at one of your GOGI workbooks or book. What suggestions do you make to him? ____

____

____

____

____

____

INCREASING MY PEACE – ACCOUNTABILITY BOX

DO YOU WANT CREDIT FOR THIS COURSE? REMEMBER TO KEEP TRACK OF YOUR DAILY STUDY BY COMPLETING THE INFORMATION BELOW TO GET YOUR CREDIT.

The month is________________; The day is ______________; The year is________; Solo study or group? ____________

Day 7 – SO, WHAT IF...

Poor planning is the biggest cause for defeat. To win, you must plan and prepare to win. You must practice to win. This goes for sports, skills, and even decision-making. Those who practice making positive decisions while in prison are usually better equipped to make positive decisions upon their release. But, life is unfair and often unkind and sometimes those individuals who have worked very hard get dealt tough blows that no one believes they deserve. To win, is not what matters, it is HOW YOU HANDLE WHAT HAPPENS that matters the most.

When you consider the above, why do you think so many prisoners express gratitude for their GOGI Tools when they get back home and start to build a new life for themselves? Why are so many formerly incarcerated individuals grateful for the practice, the repetitive study, the calendar, and the literal boredom that comes from practice? Why do they appreciate their GOGI? ________________

____

____

____

____

Is it possible for you to consider using your GOGI Tools like you might consider practicing a sport? Or a skill like fixing a car or drawing a picture? Is it possible to consider the GOGI TOOLBOX like a skill that needs constant repetition? What might be the benefits to considering your study of GOGI like a sport or skill? ____

____

____

____

How does mastery of anything create confidence and a solid awareness of possible dangers hidden in the dark corners? ____

____

____

____

How can mastery of the GOGI Tools you are learning increase your peace through the confidence you can build? Basically, what's in it for you? ________________________________

____

____

____

____

INCREASING MY PEACE – ACCOUNTABILITY BOX

DO YOU WANT CREDIT FOR THIS COURSE? REMEMBER TO KEEP TRACK OF YOUR DAILY STUDY BY COMPLETING THE INFORMATION BELOW TO GET YOUR CREDIT.

The month is______________; The day is ______________; The year is________; Solo study or group? ____________

LIFE HAPPENS

So, JaRome is returned to your block. Turns out there was no need for alarm. JaRome isn't in danger nor will he create danger. He is not going to retaliate for his brother's killing. In fact, he returns to the block with a huge commitment to becoming a GOGI leader and taking GOGI back to the streets to help other kids break the stupid cycle of killing each other over some colored piece of fabric that has caused nothing but harm to families. Turns out the GOGI book you gave him was his sole source of reading and he knows he can be a solution, rather than part of the problem. He is moved in with Rico. Odd fit, but whatever works. The new C.O. pops open your doors and lets you meet in the dayroom with JaRome and Rico.

Knowing what you know about JaRome and Rico, what assignment can you give them so they begin to learn more about the GOGI Tools? How do you introduce Rico to JaRome? ____________

*How can you set JaRome on a course that will help him in his goal to represent his community in a new and more powerful way?*____________

As you begin to work with these two men, you start to think about this whole "GOGI" thing and you get ideas. What are some of your ideas? ____________

Today I can... ____________

Tomorrow I can... ____________

*In the future I could...*____________

I know that I... ____________

This is art is a gift to GOGI from Keith E.

DO YOU WANT CREDIT FOR THIS COURSE? REMEMBER TO KEEP TRACK OF YOUR DAILY STUDY BY COMPLETING THE INFORMATION BELOW TO GET YOUR CREDIT.

The month is______________; The day is ______________; The year is________; Solo study or group? ____________

Week 6

INCREASING YOUR PEACE BY USING TOOLS OF THE BODY

Day 1 – TOOLS OF THE BODY

You already know the GOGI Tools were created by prisoners for other prisoners. Each tool was a gift to GOGI during the period when GOGI was becoming what it is today. The first tool was created in 2002 and the last tool was added to the GOGI TOOLBOX in 2009.

There are four different groups of tools. These are different types of tools that usually help in different situations. Much like the different types of tools you use to fix a car, build a house, or the different types of tools that might be used to put on makeup or do hair. Each tool has a different function, and similar tools can be grouped together.

The section of tools you have learned during the previous three weeks of study belong to the section of tools called the TOOLS OF THE BODY. The prisoners who created these tools realized that in many cases, they needed simple tools to control their body, and to redirect their impulses, addictions, or old habits.

*Write down what you believe to be the most important part of the three paragraphs above. What strikes you as information you might share with someone about your GOGI studies?*____________

When GOGI refers to the GOGI TOOLS as belonging to "sections" and serving specific functions, does that remind you of any tools you use to complete certain tasks? When you eat, are there different tools for different tasks? What about art and drawing? What about your clothing? Are there different types of clothing for different tasks? When you look at the GOGI TOOLS and specifically the TOOLS OF THE BODY, you may be able to see the perfection in what the prisoners have created. You have BOSS OF MY BRAIN, BELLY BREATHING, and FIVE SECOND LIGHTSWITCH.

When it comes to anger, rage, frustration, and even depression or anxiety, how do you think the TOOLS OF THE BODY can be useful to just about anyone? ____________________

INCREASING MY PEACE – ACCOUNTABILITY BOX

DO YOU WANT CREDIT FOR THIS COURSE? REMEMBER TO KEEP TRACK OF YOUR DAILY STUDY BY COMPLETING THE INFORMATION BELOW TO GET YOUR CREDIT.

The month is________________; The day is ______________; The year is________; Solo study or group? ____________

LIFE HAPPENS

This is YOUR chance to write a scenario using BOSS OF MY BRAIN. You can write something that happened to you. Or you can write something that you witnessed happen to someone else. Or you can make up a story, just for the fun of it.

The only requirement is that somewhere in the story your main character avoids rage, anger, and frustration by using his/her tool called BOSS OF MY BRAIN.

Here are some helpful hints on writing a scenario. It helps to create a better story if your main character has a critical decision to make and your reader just is not sure which way the character will go. You know, because this is YOUR story, that your main character will use BOSS OF MY BRAIN and in the end all will be OK. But the reader won't know this until your main character makes that choice and whips out his BOSS OF MY BRAIN tool.

What story would you like to tell? Write your story here. If you choose not to write a story, just write the words I am BOSS OF MY BRAIN 50 times and fill the lines on the page. ________________

DO YOU WANT CREDIT FOR THIS COURSE? REMEMBER TO KEEP TRACK OF YOUR DAILY STUDY BY COMPLETING THE INFORMATION BELOW TO GET YOUR CREDIT.

The month is________________; The day is ______________; The year is________; Solo study or group? ____________

Day 2 – WHO'S YOUR BOSS?

Only you can be the boss of your own brain. Only you can tell your brain what to do. You are your boss, even if you are a bad boss and you let your brain do whatever it does automatically. No one is the boss over what you think, what you feel, and what opinions you choose to have. Only you are the boss of your brain.

What do you think about the idea that you are the boss of your own brain even if you are a bad boss?

____

____

What do you think and how do you feel when you read that you are the boss of your brain, even if you are a bad boss? Does that make you feel angry? Do you have a long line of excuses about why your brain is not under your control? ______________________________

____

____

____

____

Many people choose to blame others for "making them" mad. When they blame others for their anger, they are actually giving their power away. They are admitting that the other person controls them and has the power to control how they feel and how they act and react. Usually the person who loses their temper is actually in the weakest position, and they may become loud or violent to try to regain power. In actuality, the angry and violent person often trades this temporary "power" for less respect and less trust from others. They are actually the person who is the most controlled.

In thinking of the violent or angry people you know, do you find that they blame others for their anger? Does that seem powerful to you? Or is it a sign of weakness? ______________________

____

____

____

____

*What are the options a person might have other than violence and anger?*___________________

____

____

____

____

INCREASING MY PEACE – ACCOUNTABILITY BOX

DO YOU WANT CREDIT FOR THIS COURSE? REMEMBER TO KEEP TRACK OF YOUR DAILY STUDY BY COMPLETING THE INFORMATION BELOW TO GET YOUR CREDIT.

The month is________________; The day is ______________; The year is_________; Solo study or group? ______________

LIFE HAPPENS

Prison has its own politics and unwritten rules about who is who and what is what. There is a fine line between not making trouble and being labeled as "weak" for not reacting to violence with more violence. Within most prisons the person who is the most violent and most angry is able to control others who simply want to be peaceful and mind their own business and work their way back home to family and friends. Anger and violence has been a part of the prison culture for as long as there have been prisons. Prisoners have suffered from this culture of violence and many have lost the chance to ever go home when they get sucked into the cycle of violence on the yard. It is a known fact that maintaining a peaceful life while in prison is one of the most difficult choices and challenges an individual can make.

Below you get to write what you think might happen if violence and anger were not a part of the prison politics. While it may seem impossible to ever happen, just for a few paragraphs let your mind wander a little bit into a new possibility. What good could come out of prisoners learning to live together more peacefully? Do you think families would benefit? Do you think loved ones and friends would benefit? ____

____

If violence were not a part of prison, then... ____

____

____

____

*Let's have you fast forward 100 years and see a GOGI "prison" where people who have harmed others or broken the rules are sent until they are no longer a danger to others. Pretend you are there. 100 years from today. You are at this place. There is no violence. What do you see? What is it like? What are the prisoners doing? How are they preparing to go home?*________________

____

In 100 years, I see... ____

____

____

____

The prisoners are... ____

____

____

____

INCREASING MY PEACE – ACCOUNTABILITY BOX

DO YOU WANT CREDIT FOR THIS COURSE? REMEMBER TO KEEP TRACK OF YOUR DAILY STUDY BY COMPLETING THE INFORMATION BELOW TO GET YOUR CREDIT.

The month is________________; The day is ______________; The year is________; Solo study or group? ____________

Day 3 – MASTERY OF YOUR TOOLS

While most anger management courses teach about anger, at GOGI we focus on ways you can move beyond the anger into a response or a thought that is more positive. In this course so far, you have learned BOSS OF MY BRAIN and then BELLY BREATHING. You then learned FIVE SECOND LIGHTSWITCH. Of these three, which do you believe might come in handy when a feeling of anger begins to creep into your awareness? Why do you think this tool may be helpful? ______________

____

____

____

If you were to try to explain BOSS OF MY BRAIN to someone who was angry, what might you say? If they were willing to listen to you, how would you describe the tool BOSS OF MY BRAIN? ______

____

____

____

Let's say they want to hear more. They are a little less angry but they want to have the peace that you enjoy. You tell them about BELLY BREATHING: ______________________________

____

What do you tell them? ____

____

____

How do you demonstrate how to make sure they are BELLY BREATHING? ______________

____

____

Finally, they have decided that getting angry just weakens them (you didn't even have to say a word) and now they have asked why you are always choosing POSITIVE ACTIONS even when people around you are getting upset. You describe how you use your FIVE SECOND LIGHTSWITCH. What do you say? ______________________________

____

____

____

____

INCREASING MY PEACE – ACCOUNTABILITY BOX

DO YOU WANT CREDIT FOR THIS COURSE? REMEMBER TO KEEP TRACK OF YOUR DAILY STUDY BY COMPLETING THE INFORMATION BELOW TO GET YOUR CREDIT.

The month is_______________; The day is _______________; The year is__________; Solo study or group? ___________

LIFE HAPPENS

Let's say that you are able to go back in time and reeducate the younger version of you. Knowing what you now know, having been through what you have been through, seeing all you have seen, let's take a moment and let you give your younger self some schooling...

Dear Younger me,

I know you think you know a lot, but let me share with you some things: ______________________

Learning that I could use tools to deal with my frustration and anger when I was your age might have changed things for me. Instead of being where I am right now, I probably would be: ________

You think your friends are important and what they do is OK for you to do. But let me share a few thoughts with you, younger me. What I would really like you to do is: ____________________

What I want you to remember is: ______________________________

With Love,

*Sign here*________________________________

(You in a few years)

INCREASING MY PEACE – ACCOUNTABILITY BOX

DO YOU WANT CREDIT FOR THIS COURSE? REMEMBER TO KEEP TRACK OF YOUR DAILY STUDY BY COMPLETING THE INFORMATION BELOW TO GET YOUR CREDIT.

The month is________________; The day is ______________; The year is________; Solo study or group? ____________

Day 4 – TOOLS OF THE BODY

The GOGI TOOLS OF THE BODY are easily taught to children ages two to eight. Why do you think these tools work so well for children of this age? Your opinion is important. This is not a question answered by any GOGI materials. This is your own perception of why these tools are easily learned and applied by kids two to eight years old. ______________________________

____

____

____

If you had been taught the GOGI TOOLS OF THE BODY each and every time you got angry when you were two to eight years old, do you think you would process your anger differently now? What would be different? ______________________________

____

____

____

It has been proven scientifically that the human brain can learn new things and that humans can adjust and adapt to things, if they apply themselves. This means that you could actually CHANGE your reactions and responses to things through practice. You COULD respond in a peaceful manner to all things by practicing your use of the GOGI TOOLS OF THE BODY. What would stand in your way of increasing your peace? ______________________________

____

____

____

*One GOGI student said that not getting angry made him feel as if he was "giving up." His peer mentor stated that there was a difference between "giving up" and "not getting sucked in." What does this mean to you and how does this relate to the subject of anger?*______________________________

____

What is "giving up?" ______________________________

____

What is not "getting sucked in?" ______________________________

*Which is possibly a more positive decision?*______________________________

____

INCREASING MY PEACE – ACCOUNTABILITY BOX

DO YOU WANT CREDIT FOR THIS COURSE? REMEMBER TO KEEP TRACK OF YOUR DAILY STUDY BY COMPLETING THE INFORMATION BELOW TO GET YOUR CREDIT.

The month is________________; The day is ______________; The year is________; Solo study or group? ____________

LIFE HAPPENS

Life does not offer a big eraser to erase things we would rather not have done or experienced. But life does keep moving forward, even if we remain stuck in the past. It has been said by thousands of people that the GOGI Tools have helped them deal with the past better so they feel as if they can move forward.

Can you relate to what they say? How or why? Why not? ____________________________

____

____

What are specific ways you can increase your peace? ______________________________

____

____

People who use the GOGI TOOLS OF THE BODY state that they have a sense of peace, that with their tools their lives don't fly off the handle. They say their lives are more manageable. They say that they wish they had learned these tools as children. Do you wish you could increase your peace, too? ____

____

____

____

____

____

____

Can you relate to what they say? Why or why not? What is it about the GOGI Tools that make them so simple to use? ____

____

____

____

Why do you believe they are so effective at increasing the peace within? __________________

____

____

____

____

DO YOU WANT CREDIT FOR THIS COURSE? REMEMBER TO KEEP TRACK OF YOUR DAILY STUDY BY COMPLETING THE INFORMATION BELOW TO GET YOUR CREDIT.

The month is________________; The day is ______________; The year is________; Solo study or group? ____________

Day 5 - FLIP THE SWITCH

Your brain is made up of parts that communicate. If you think of your brain like a long line into the chow hall, you can better understand how your brain works. Let's say the first guy in line tells the guy behind him, "Hey, we have steak and lobster tonight." The next guy passes that information down the line until the entire line is expecting steak and lobster. One message travels down the line and creates quite a stir when steak and lobster is not placed onto the trays.

Your brain is similar. You may have one thought and a message goes throughout your body telling your body one thing, but it might very well turn out to be something different.

Was there ever a time when you THOUGHT something with such a firm commitment and you just KNEW it was true, but at a later date discovered that it was nothing more than being told you were getting steak and lobster for chow? Can you explain how you felt it was SO right but it ended up SO wrong? ____

____

____

____

In your study of the GOGI Tools, specifically FIVE SECOND LIGHTSWITCH, how do you think having this tool might help when you get misinformation, wrong information, no information, or the information changes up on you? ____

____

____

____

Going back to the chow line, what might happen if a guy in the middle of the line decides that he is quite certain the guy at the front of the line is wishful thinking. The guy in the middle is certain there is no steak and lobster. Instead of telling the guy behind him that steak is on its way to his dinner tray, he tells the next guy "I wonder what is on the menu." Instantly the erroneous information is stopped and half of the line is not misinformed or misguided. The middle guy might have even stopped a riot on the yard with his ability to think clearly and not follow the crowd.

Was there ever a time when you were able to stand up and make a different choice because you realized that the information you were getting was flawed? Explain what went through your mind when you decided to do something different than the crowd? Were you using FIVE SECOND LIGHTSWITCH and you didn't realize it? ____

____

____

____

INCREASING MY PEACE – ACCOUNTABILITY BOX

DO YOU WANT CREDIT FOR THIS COURSE? REMEMBER TO KEEP TRACK OF YOUR DAILY STUDY BY COMPLETING THE INFORMATION BELOW TO GET YOUR CREDIT.

The month is________________; The day is ________________; The year is________; Solo study or group? __________

LIFE HAPPENS

Let's say you have a son. You call him KC. For the past ten years in prison your ex-wife has been real good about bringing KC to see you at least once a year. Now, at fifteen years old, he is not as interested in seeing dad. He would prefer to sit at home on his phone playing games or some other such nonsense. He told your ex that he doesn't want to go to the next visit because it is too far of a drive.

You know the signs. You know he is headed down a path that leads to no good. His mother tells you on a Sunday call that he just is not the same boy she raised, and now he is staying out late and disrespecting her. His grades are steadily falling and she doesn't like the new set of friends he parades through her home at all hours of the night.

She starts to cry on the phone, asking you – begging you – to talk some sense into your son.

You are just about to ask to speak to your son who has just walked into the house.

"Take it home," the officer demands.

"Can I finish my call?" you ask nicely.

"I said take it home. Now," he says.

You have not gotten so mad so quickly for a very, very long time. You have a Board hearing next month. You can't get written up. You know you have to maintain.

What is the first GOGI Tool that comes to your mind? ______________________________

____

How can you use this tool? ____

____

____

____

What do you say to your son's mother? ________________________________

____

____

What do you say to the officer? _____________________________________

____

When the cell door slams shut and you are left with your thoughts, how do you process your anger?

____

____

DO YOU WANT CREDIT FOR THIS COURSE? REMEMBER TO KEEP TRACK OF YOUR DAILY STUDY BY COMPLETING THE INFORMATION BELOW TO GET YOUR CREDIT.

The month is__________________; The day is _______________; The year is_________; Solo study or group? _______________

Day 6 – THE POWER IN PEACE

Your GOGI Tools are going to come in very handy as you apply them to your life. The key is, you will need to apply them to your life every day. One way to do this is to open a GOGI book for two minutes every morning to remind yourself to live that day THE GOGI WAY. If you do this one thing, you will find yourself more peaceful and less angry.

Why do you think that reading for as little as two minutes each morning will help you remain more peaceful? What might you enjoy reading? ____

____

____

When your brain is trained to understand that you choose to be a peaceful person not an angry person, your emotions will change. As your brain becomes stronger, you become less angry. This is because you become wise and insightful, not reactionary and immature. As your brain becomes under YOUR control, you become more strategic about where to place your precious energy and attention. You become a master of using the tool BOSS OF MY BRAIN and, interestingly enough, you earn greater respect from the people around you.

What part of the above paragraph feels consistent with your experience? Do you know calm people who are powerful and have self-control who are respected? And, do you know hotheads who THINK they are respected but they are really just loud and annoying? When looking at your own life, are there times when you get angry when being still and powerful might be more effective? _________

____

____

____

Some people believe they were "born" to be angry, procrastinate, have a short attention span, and be lazy, and impulsive. What might you say to someone who thought they could never use the GOGI Tools simply because they stated they "fried" their brain on drugs for too many years and getting angry is just who they are? Knowing what you know about the GOGI Tools and how they were created by and for prisoners, what might you say to this person? And how can you share with them your own success with your GOGI Tools? What would you tell them? ____________________

____

____

How do the tools apply to your own life? ____

____

____

____

INCREASING MY PEACE – ACCOUNTABILITY BOX

DO YOU WANT CREDIT FOR THIS COURSE? REMEMBER TO KEEP TRACK OF YOUR DAILY STUDY BY COMPLETING THE INFORMATION BELOW TO GET YOUR CREDIT.

The month is________________; The day is ______________; The year is________; Solo study or group? __________

LIFE HAPPENS

Life happens. That is the plain truth. Sometimes it spins out of control and we get angry. And, more often than not, when we get angry things get worse – not better.

On this page you will write one scenario and describe the situation where you lost your cool or got regrettably angry at someone or something. In writing this scenario, you may find that it is likely that there were many times where you could have used a GOGI Tool and avoided many of the problems that came from anger.

Do you remember the date or around the time when anger got the best of someone you know? _____

____

____

Do you remember what made them angry? ________________________________

____

____

____

What do you think they were feeling? ________________________________

____

____

What might they have been thinking? ________________________________

____

____

____

Did they have options? ________________________________

____

____

____

Might they have made a more positive choice? ________________________________

____

____

____

INCREASING MY PEACE – ACCOUNTABILITY BOX

DO YOU WANT CREDIT FOR THIS COURSE? REMEMBER TO KEEP TRACK OF YOUR DAILY STUDY BY COMPLETING THE INFORMATION BELOW TO GET YOUR CREDIT.

The month is__________________; The day is ________________; The year is________; Solo study or group? ______________

Day 7 – Recap and Review

Write the three TOOLS OF THE BODY

1) ____

2) ____

3) ____

What are the keywords for these tools?

1) ____

2) ____

3) ____

What weeks of the year do most GOGI students study these tools?

BOSS OF MY BRAIN	BELLY BREATHING	FIVE SECOND LIGHTSWITCH
_____ week of _______ month	_____ week of _______ month	_____ week of _______ month
_____ week of _______ month	_____ week of _______ month	_____ week of _______ month
_____ week of _______ month	_____ week of _______ month	_____ week of _______ month
_____ week of _______ month	_____ week of _______ month	_____ week of _______ month

What do you like about one of these tools? ______________________________

____

*How might one of these tools help you in making the most positive decisions?*______________

____

*When you think of GOGI TOOLS, what comes to mind?*______________________

____

Why do you think the course must be repetitive? ______________________

____

How might TOOLS OF THE BODY help you to INCREASE YOUR PEACE? ____________

____

____

____

This art is a gift to GOGI from Jeremy B.

DO YOU WANT CREDIT FOR THIS COURSE? REMEMBER TO KEEP TRACK OF YOUR DAILY STUDY BY COMPLETING THE INFORMATION BELOW TO GET YOUR CREDIT.

The month is________________; The day is ______________; The year is________; Solo study or group? ____________

Week 7

INCREASING YOUR PEACE APPLYING YOUR NEW TOOLS

Day 1 – THE NEW COOL

While you may not believe it, and while it may not seem true for your life experience, there are many, MANY people who believe that people who lose their temper, people who are violent, and people who cannot control their negative emotions are weak. For many people, a sign of weakness is raising of the voice, yelling, cursing, hitting, or harming others. For many people, it is a sign of true strength when bad things happen and the individual can maintain total and complete control over their emotions. When most people on this earth see someone who is violent, they do not respect them, they do not think they are cool, and they do not perceive that person to be successful or powerful at all.

When you read the above paragraph, did you grow up like most people or did you grow up with the misconception that angry outbursts were in some way a sign of strength? ________________

____

____

Can you understand how most people on this planet have very little respect for those who cannot control themselves in all situations? ________________________________

____

One man who had killed another human being out of a "duty" he felt and to "protect" his reputation. After serving more than ten years of his 25 year sentence, he stated that how any person responds to emotions is a measure of maturity and the ability to see beyond the immediate. He stated that he now knows he always HAD a choice, he just did not see the choice at that time.

*Do you really believe that the man in the above situation had a "duty" to kill another person? Do you believe he had no choice, or do you believe he was not willing to choose the "difficult" choice? What is the difference between "no choice" and making the more difficult choice?*__________________

____

____

Is it possible to change the prison system (and your community and family and yourself) if you rely upon violence and anger to solve problems? Or do you think that violence will need to be replaced by increasing the peace and finding a more mature way to deal with situations? ______________

____

____

____

INCREASING MY PEACE – ACCOUNTABILITY BOX

DO YOU WANT CREDIT FOR THIS COURSE? REMEMBER TO KEEP TRACK OF YOUR DAILY STUDY BY COMPLETING THE INFORMATION BELOW TO GET YOUR CREDIT.

The month is________________; The day is ______________; The year is________; Solo study or group? __________

LIFE HAPPENS

Write down the specifics of one thing that made you angry when you were 15 years old? What was that thing? ____

____

____

*Looking back at that thing that made you mad when you were 15, does it seem as important now as it did then? Does getting angry about that thing seem like something you would do now?*__________

____

____

*The thing about anger is that with a little distance the thing you were angry about does not seem as important, or, at the very least your need to react or retaliate or act out does not seem so important. Why do you think that is true for most people?*____________________________

____

____

____

You have a tool now called BOSS OF MY BRAIN. You know that you have a SMART PART, an EMOTIONAL PART, and an OLD HABIT PART. How can use of this tool help you see beyond the immediate to the long-term outcome of your reaction? ______________________

____

____

____

If you grew up in an environment where increasing your peace was the sign of being an adult, powerful, and respected, do you think there would also be less drug use and drinking around you?

____

____

*Why do you think more people become violent when they drink or use drugs? Do you think it is because drugs and alcohol weaken your ability to make good decisions? If increasing your peace is a sign of maturity, what does drinking and drug use mean to you?*______________________

____

____

____

INCREASING MY PEACE – ACCOUNTABILITY BOX

DO YOU WANT CREDIT FOR THIS COURSE? REMEMBER TO KEEP TRACK OF YOUR DAILY STUDY BY COMPLETING THE INFORMATION BELOW TO GET YOUR CREDIT.

The month is_______________; The day is ______________; The year is_______; Solo study or group? __________

Day 2 – THE BIG LIE

Some people get angry when they feel as if things are not going the way they want them to go. When things go "wrong" some people want to regain or establish control. When they can't control things, they get angry. Anger and rage has more to do with control than anything else. And, temper tantrums and violence provide the illusion of control, but this type of control is only temporary. It often leads to more violence and anger because in truth, we cannot control what goes on in the mind of another human. We can only temporarily control their behavior when we act out. We cannot control their heart or mind through intimidation or fear. When we act out, we push them and others even further away and this creates more anger. It is a loop of failure to control.

What do you think about the above information? Does it "feel" as if it might be true? Do you see how anger and violence only offers the illusion of control, it does not change the hearts and minds of others? How can your BELLY BREATHING tool help you to understand the information in the above paragraph? ______________________________

____

____

____

It is a lie that physical actions can truly control others. It cannot control them in their minds and hearts where the important stuff is kept private; it can only keep their physical body in a place for a little while, for as long as you are acting out. But the second you are not there to wield the illusion of control, the individual is free to feel and believe what they wish to believe. You cannot control their minds.

What do you think about the lie that anger and violence actually "control" things? Do you think it would make life better if you surrounded yourself with individuals who understood the lie of anger? That anger and violence does not really change much for the better? ____________________

____

____

____

____

How can your BELLY BREATHING tool help you avoid the lie and increase your peace? __________

____

____

____

____

____

INCREASING MY PEACE – ACCOUNTABILITY BOX

DO YOU WANT CREDIT FOR THIS COURSE? REMEMBER TO KEEP TRACK OF YOUR DAILY STUDY BY COMPLETING THE INFORMATION BELOW TO GET YOUR CREDIT.

The month is________________; The day is ______________; The year is________; Solo study or group? __________

LIFE HAPPENS

True story. Kevin is a real person. He shared in his GOGI Group that his childhood was filled with things he could not control and his mother tried to control him with beatings, which never controlled him for very long.

He started selling little dime bags first so he could buy new shoes like all the other kids. One thing led to the next and he robbed his first bank. In his GOGI Group he was open and honest, as most GOGI Groups become over time. He stated that he loved the "control" he had when he went into the bank with a gun and demanded that everyone get on the floor. He got a huge "rush" that was better than any high he could ever achieve. The control he wished he had as a child, he believed he could achieve when he walked into the bank and people started screaming and he ordered them to lay down and "shut the f--- up!" Even as he was telling the story the members of the group could see him getting excited. He told the men in his group that it all happened before he knew it, the rush just took over.

As he told his story, one of the more mature Men of GOGI was quiet and then simply asked, "Kev, how is that working out for you?"

The rest of the men in the group chuckled a little. Kevin was silent for a moment.

What is the illusion - the lie - that Kevin believes? ____________________________

____

____

What would you recommend for Kevin as he learns more about controlling his life by increasing his levels of peace? ____

____

____

When someone has impulse challenges like Kevin, when they move too fast to think things out, what GOGI Tool might be helpful to them? ________________________________

____

____

____

Let's say your goal is to help them so they get a few moments to think before acting out. What tool might you teach them and why? ______________________________________

____

____

____

INCREASING MY PEACE – ACCOUNTABILITY BOX

DO YOU WANT CREDIT FOR THIS COURSE? REMEMBER TO KEEP TRACK OF YOUR DAILY STUDY BY COMPLETING THE INFORMATION BELOW TO GET YOUR CREDIT.

The month is_______________; The day is _______________; The year is________; Solo study or group? __________

Day 3 – MOVE IT TO LOSE IT

One way to get beyond the illusion and lie that violence or anger provides any lasting control, is to move away from the place or person as quickly as you can (FIVE SECOND LIGHTSWITCH: get to a POSITIVE ACTION). When you are not in the face of the situation and you can become active with exercise or walking or sit-ups or arm curls or anything else that gets your body in moving, you will find less anger boiling inside you. (BELLY BREATHING) The FEELINGS of anger can be overwhelming and very real, but your reactions do not need to be violence and rage. Moving away from the person or situation oftentimes is enough for you to control your situation (BOSS OF MY BRAIN).

Getting your heart rate up even just a few beats through physical movement forces your body to take in more oxygen. Getting more oxygen to your brain helps you think clearly. When you move your body away from the situation you lose the immediate urgency to react. This is when the BELLY BREATHING tool comes in handy. Exercise requires that you take in more oxygen, and oxygen can change your mind about things. When you move your body away from the immediate situation you often lose the impulse for acting out. When you move it, you lose it.

Explain, based on what you have learned, how BELLY BREATHING helps anyone move away from an old habit, immature reaction, or harmful response to a more mature and peaceful way to control life. ____

____

____

Here is something pretty deep for you to consider. For many people in prison, the person who moves away from an altercation is looked down upon and called names. How mature does that sound to you as you read this? Is it mature to almost "force" people into violence? You may say that "that is just how prison is." Here are some questions for you:

Who made the rule that you are weak when you choose to increase the peace on a yard? Who made that rule? And, more importantly, why do prisoners buy into that lie? ____________________

____

____

Who will be brave enough to change that rule? How many prisoners would it take to start a class-action lawsuit against all prisoners who force violence to be the lifestyle? ____________________

____

Realistically, how is the prison system ever going to change when the unwritten rule is that you can't respond maturely to someone who can't manage their own anger? ____________________

____

What needs to happen for PEACE to be the new COOL on the prison yard? ____________________

____

INCREASING MY PEACE – ACCOUNTABILITY BOX

DO YOU WANT CREDIT FOR THIS COURSE? REMEMBER TO KEEP TRACK OF YOUR DAILY STUDY BY COMPLETING THE INFORMATION BELOW TO GET YOUR CREDIT.

The month is________________; The day is ______________; The year is________; Solo study or group? __________

LIFE HAPPENS

Let's imagine a prison yard that is entirely, completely, and unwaveringly dedicated to training prisoners to become powerful peace promoters when they are returned to their communities. What if this place, this "GOGI Prison" was all about training community leaders who could live humble lives of service, helping children to see how important it is to be a good, kind, and loving person?

Someone a very long time ago decided that prisons needed to be violent and everyone bought into that rule. The prisoners bought into that rule. The cops bought into that rule. The community bought into that rule. Everyone bought into that rule.

Why can't that rule be changed? Who was that person who made that rule and do you really think it is the only choice available? ____

____

____

Imagine in your mind what might happen if every prisoner decided, today, that the old rule didn't work anymore. That violence didn't really make communities any healthier or happier. That violence didn't really control anything for long, and it simply gave the cops permission to lockdown the yard. Would you choose a "GOGI Prison" over the place where you now find yourself? Why? __________

____

____

____

____

The funny thing about humans is that they usually follow the leader and then complain that the leader is not doing a good job. What would it take for prisoners to simply decide to eliminate all violence in all prisons as a means of control? ____________________

____

____

____

____

*How could the sharing of GOGI Tools help change the culture in prisons? Would that help you in your life? Why or why not?*________________________________

____

____

____

INCREASING MY PEACE – ACCOUNTABILITY BOX

DO YOU WANT CREDIT FOR THIS COURSE? REMEMBER TO KEEP TRACK OF YOUR DAILY STUDY BY COMPLETING THE INFORMATION BELOW TO GET YOUR CREDIT.

The month is_________________; The day is _______________; The year is_________; Solo study or group? ______________

Day 4 – WRITE IT DOWN

It is likely that if you are in prison you have a lot of things in your life for which you are angry. It might be something that happened to you. It might be how you were treated. It might be how you were raised. It might be a million and one things that were unfair or downright wrong, things that never should happen to any human being.

Anger sometimes gets bottled up inside us and then, out of nowhere, it seems to explode. Sometimes, when there is a lot of anger stuffed inside, it may seem as if you had absolutely no other choice, but to hit or yell or in some other way explode to let some of that anger out.

We ALL have things in our life that deserved our anger, but none of those things deserve to keep us angry.

While many adults experienced many forms of abuse as children, some people, especially men, may not feel comfortable discussing emotional, physical, or sexual abuse they experienced. For that reason, many men simply write down a word or a name to represent things like this. They might put "Uncle Joe" on a line and only they know what that means. Write down four things that totally deserved your anger in the past, but that no longer deserve to keep you angry today.

1) ____

2) ____

3) ____

4) ____

I ____________________________ acknowledge that the above things got me angry, but I know they do not deserve to KEEP ME ANGRY. I want to INCREASE MY PEACE today and will not let these things keep me angry any longer.

Signed ______________________________

Your name

*Write down the GOGI Tool you will use to INCREASE YOUR PEACE and why that tool will work for you.*____

____

____

Why is learning GOGI so repetitive? ______________________________

____

____

____

INCREASING MY PEACE – ACCOUNTABILITY BOX

DO YOU WANT CREDIT FOR THIS COURSE? REMEMBER TO KEEP TRACK OF YOUR DAILY STUDY BY COMPLETING THE INFORMATION BELOW TO GET YOUR CREDIT.

The month is______________; The day is ______________; The year is________; Solo study or group? __________

LIFE HAPPENS

One Man of GOGI stated that "yes, life happens, but now it happens on MY terms." *What does that mean to you?* ______________________________

This man does not get any write-ups from the cops for acting out like he did when he first came to prison as a young man. Does that mean that everything goes his way? Does it mean that he is in control of things outside himself? ______________________________

The man stated that until he studied and learned his GOGI Tools, and until he could see the bigger picture about his potential to be helpful instead of harmful to society, he was angry and violent. To deal with his anger and violence he drank. Once he started to learn his GOGI Tools, he drank less and could better manage his anger. What positive changes will the GOGI Tools make in your life?

What he states is a common theme for men in prison. They drink or use drugs to help with their anger. It's almost as if drinking gives them a moment to forget how messed up things are. Do you see how this can become a lie that is destructive? What do you think about this lie? _______________

INCREASING MY PEACE – ACCOUNTABILITY BOX

DO YOU WANT CREDIT FOR THIS COURSE? REMEMBER TO KEEP TRACK OF YOUR DAILY STUDY BY COMPLETING THE INFORMATION BELOW TO GET YOUR CREDIT.

The month is__________________; The day is ________________; The year is__________; Solo study or group? ______________

Day 5 – WHY BOTHER?

Prison tends to be a place of anger, a place of "why bother" to try harder or do things differently. This attitude can increase the levels of anger in anyone, and for good reason. So, if the general attitude in prison is "why bother" then is there any wonder why there is so much violence in the lives of prisoners?

Why do you think many people in prison are able to resist the "why bother" attitude by increasing their peace and making different decisions in their daily life? ______________________________

____

____

Do you think it is because the situation seems so hopeless? Do you think it is peer pressure? Do you think it is "just the way things are in prison"? Or is it a combination of all these things and more? ___

____

____

____

There is one prison that has a solid track record of paroling lifers and giving them their freedom. More lifers go home from that prison than any other prison in that state. The lifers are getting out and only one percent of them ever get rearrested. They are in society and living good lives and being of service to others.

When speaking with a group of prisoners at a prison that does not parole any lifers, the GOGI Coach said, "If you can, get yourself to XXX prison. Guys go home from XXX prison." Two men on the bench started to laugh and said "XXX prison? We aren't going there. Those men are soft."

In your opinion, how is this attitude part of the problem? How does this attitude of being "soft" keep men locked up? ____

____

____

What might it take for these men to realize that the men getting out are "free" from the angry prison mentality that keeps them sitting on that bench? ______________________________

____

____

What might it take for them to rethink who the REAL men are? How are these men buying into the lie that violence and anger make a 'real' man? ______________________________

____

INCREASING MY PEACE – ACCOUNTABILITY BOX

DO YOU WANT CREDIT FOR THIS COURSE? REMEMBER TO KEEP TRACK OF YOUR DAILY STUDY BY COMPLETING THE INFORMATION BELOW TO GET YOUR CREDIT.

The month is________________; The day is ______________; The year is________; Solo study or group? ___________

LIFE HAPPENS

Here are some scenarios for you to consider:

1) Your counselor meets with you and tells you your release date is changed. They miscalculated your time and you won't be getting out March 21st in time for your daughter's graduation from high school. Instead, you will be released the following YEAR!!!!

What tool do you use and why?

Circle one and explain:

BOSS OF MY BRAIN *BELLY BREATHING* *FIVE SECOND LIGHTSWITCH*

2) The same day when you call home to tell them about your release date, your mom tells you your sister got arrested for drug possession. She is given two years prison time because she walked off a previous drug program and the judge is done with her. Your niece and nephew are put into foster care because your mom is on probation. Your mom tells you this means she can't keep her kids because after 18 months they go up for adoption. Mom cries. You go out onto the yard and you see your sister's co-defendant, the very guy who gives your sister her stuff. He is now on your yard. He is the very guy who won't listen and leave your family alone. You have an overwhelming need to beat the "heck" out of this guy.

What tool do you use and why?

Circle one and explain:

BOSS OF MY BRAIN *BELLY BREATHING* *FIVE SECOND LIGHTSWITCH*

INCREASING MY PEACE – ACCOUNTABILITY BOX

DO YOU WANT CREDIT FOR THIS COURSE? REMEMBER TO KEEP TRACK OF YOUR DAILY STUDY BY COMPLETING THE INFORMATION BELOW TO GET YOUR CREDIT.

The month is________________; The day is ______________; The year is________; Solo study or group? ___________

Day 6 – IF NOT ANGRY, WHO ARE YOU?

Many people define themselves by their behavior. If this is true, then might you be defining yourself as "angry" or someone with a hot temper? If you define yourself this way, does it seem logical that you would live up to your definition?

When people make the choice to do things differently, it sometimes creates discomfort and uncertainty. Humans don't like discomfort, so we often remain just as we are, even if we are miserable. Angry people remain angry because they are afraid of what it would be like to be something else.

How can using your GOGI Tools help you try out a new way of being without putting you on blast for the world to criticize or judge? ____

____

____

How can you use your GOGI Tools in a small way every day to build your comfort level in increasing your internal peace? ____

____

____

Why do you think it is easier to start with small changes and practice new ways of being in a smaller and more controlled situation? ____

____

____

____

Many Men of GOGI state that they had to learn tools that helped them increase their levels of peace before they could feel comfortable making changes. They also state that once they started using their tools, and once they practiced them every day, it got easier to become more peaceful.

Why do you think so many prisoners are finding that their GOGI Tools help them gradually change their lives for the better? ____

____

____

____

Again, why do you think learning The GOGI Tools requires you to write the same things over and over again? ____

____

____

INCREASING MY PEACE – ACCOUNTABILITY BOX

DO YOU WANT CREDIT FOR THIS COURSE? REMEMBER TO KEEP TRACK OF YOUR DAILY STUDY BY COMPLETING THE INFORMATION BELOW TO GET YOUR CREDIT.

The month is________________; The day is ______________; The year is________; Solo study or group? ____________

LIFE HAPPENS

Here are two scenarios. In each scenario, please circle how old you think the person is and write down why you think they are that age. Write down what GOGI Tool they could have used or what tool they likely used in their situation.

Keep in mind that facts prove most people "age out" of crime and violence. At some point they realize that all the "runnin' and gunnin'" is a big waste of time and they start making different choices with their life. They become less concerned with what others think about them and more concerned with increasing their levels of peace.

Delvonte: Delvonte knew he was going to prison, even when he was a kid. That is because 90 percent of the men in his community served at least one prison term. Prison was a rite of passage, the way you showed you were a "man" in his neighborhood. In fact, the rougher the prison, the more of a man you must be.

Someone on the yard said something he didn't like. Delvonte was disrespected. He wasn't going to put up with that and he walked over to the guy who was in his corner of the yard and hit him, and kept hitting until the cops took him to the ground and cuffed him up. He was happy to see sufficient blood on the guy and he knew he had done what needed to be done. The cops had forced everyone down on the yard, putting all of them with their faces in the dust while the cops cleaned up the situation. Delvonte got written up, was sent to administrative segregation and then was transferred.

How old is Delvonte? Circle one: 24 years old or 42 years old. How can you guess his age?

____

What tools could Delvonte have used to avoid a write-up and being sent to AdSeg and then moved?

____

____

Juan: Juan didn't doubt he would land in prison, even as a kid. After all, his dad and all three brothers served prison terms. He started to wonder if this was all there was to his life, if there was no chance for something better. His new cellie got a job in the kitchen and is making some solid pruno and wants to share it with Juan. Juan decides it's time for him to do things differently. He is done with the game. It's just not – well, he can't really put a word to it. He just does not want to die living this life. He puts in for a transfer to any prison that has GOGI programming.

How old is Juan? Circle one: 24 years old or 42 years old? How can you guess his age?

____

What tools did Juan use to make his decision? ______________________________

____

____

INCREASING MY PEACE – ACCOUNTABILITY BOX

DO YOU WANT CREDIT FOR THIS COURSE? REMEMBER TO KEEP TRACK OF YOUR DAILY STUDY BY COMPLETING THE INFORMATION BELOW TO GET YOUR CREDIT.

The month is________________; The day is ______________; The year is_______; Solo study or group? ____________

Day 7 – Recap and Review

*Repetition creates habits. How long do you think you will need to repeat your GOGI Tools before they become habits and why?*______________________________

____

____

____

What other positive habits do you have and how long did they take to develop? ____________

____

____

____

What weeks of the year do most GOGI students study these tools?

BOSS OF MY BRAIN	BELLY BREATHING	FIVE SECOND LIGHTSWITCH
____ week of ______ month	____ week of ______ month	____ week of ______ month
____ week of ______ month	____ week of ______ month	____ week of ______ month
____ week of ______ month	____ week of ______ month	____ week of ______ month
____ week of ______ month	____ week of ______ month	____ week of ______ month

*How might one of these tools help you in making the most positive decisions?*____________

____

*When you think of GOGI TOOLS, what comes to mind?*______________________

____

If someone told you GOGI seemed too simple to work, what would you tell them? __________

____

____

____

____

____

____

____

Whats your identity?

my new print.

Change your identity!

By Dustin Jeffries

INCREASING MY PEACE – ACCOUNTABILITY BOX

DO YOU WANT CREDIT FOR THIS COURSE? REMEMBER TO KEEP TRACK OF YOUR DAILY STUDY BY COMPLETING THE INFORMATION BELOW TO GET YOUR CREDIT.

The month is________________; The day is ______________; The year is________; Solo study or group? ____________

Week 8

INCREASING YOUR PEACE AND MOVING FORWARD WITH YOUR LIFE

Day 1 – MOVING FORWARD

Have you read about these tools in this book yet? If not, you are cheating yourself of important information that will help you be the best version of you. Before you start with this week's study, please do yourself a favor and take a moment to read about these tools in this and other GOGI books. Then, continue with today's study.

Anger is something from which you can move forward. You do not need to let anger control you. And, when you use your GOGI Tools, you have within you the ability to move forward and leave anger in the dust.

This is your last week in this INCREASING YOUR PEACE: Anger Management The GOGI Way course. But, this does not mean that you need to stop learning and growing and increasing your levels of peace each day.

Have you enjoyed this course? Has it been helpful to you in your efforts to increase your levels of peace? How has it helped you? ____

____

____

When courses end, some people think the learning is over. They believe the lie that they are supposed to be "done" and "get it" and that if they do not succeed, it is because the course didn't work or that they are stupid, or can't change.

Why do you think GOGI is different? Why do you think that GOGI encourages you to continue to practice, and even repeat this course over and over again? ______________________

____

____

GOGI was created by prisoners for other prisoners. How does that make it easier for prisoners to learn the tools? ____

____

____

One Man of GOGI stated that he was "GOGI-4-Life." In your opinion, what does this mean? Do you think someone who practices these tools every day is more likely to increase their peace? ________

____

INCREASING MY PEACE – ACCOUNTABILITY BOX

DO YOU WANT CREDIT FOR THIS COURSE? REMEMBER TO KEEP TRACK OF YOUR DAILY STUDY BY COMPLETING THE INFORMATION BELOW TO GET YOUR CREDIT.

The month is________________; The day is ______________; The year is________; Solo study or group? ____________

LIFE HAPPENS

Your life will go on beyond this course. And, your life will have as much peace as you create through the choices you make. The tools you have had the opportunity to learn in this course are now yours to use, or yours to tuck away and forget.

In this section, you have the opportunity to write down some of the choices you can make that will increase your levels of peace long after you turn in this workbook for the credit you have earned. What are three things you can do in the coming weeks or months that will permit you to increase your own levels of peace?

1. To increase my peace I can... ______________________________

____

____

2. I can also... ______________________________

____

*3. Finally, I can...*______________________________

____

____

How might you continue to expand and grow in your awareness that anger and violence are choices but not the ONLY choices? What are three things you can do to remind yourself that there are other choices for you?

1. I can remind myself by... ______________________________

____

____

____

2. I can also... ______________________________

____

____

*3. Finally, I can...*______________________________

____

____

____

INCREASING MY PEACE – ACCOUNTABILITY BOX

DO YOU WANT CREDIT FOR THIS COURSE? REMEMBER TO KEEP TRACK OF YOUR DAILY STUDY BY COMPLETING THE INFORMATION BELOW TO GET YOUR CREDIT.

The month is________________; The day is ________________; The year is__________; Solo study or group? ____________

Day 2 – ARE YOU YOUR PAST?

At GOGI we believe that you are only your past if you want to remain defined by your past. At GOGI we believe that you can choose today to experience your life without the heavy weight of what happened to you or what you did.

At GOGI we separate the past from the present and let you use your tools today to make the positive choices you did not make in the past. Without the baggage of the past there is no excuse for making bad decisions. A bad decision is your choice, rather than an automatic and uncontrollable response. Choosing to become angry and act out is your choice today. Similarly, choosing to increase your peace is also your choice. You are not your past with GOGI. You are your choices today.

What do you think when you read the above? Is it possible that you are not your past? Is it possible that today you can define yourself by today's decisions? What does that mean for the level of peace you can create in your life? ____

____

____

____

If anger or violence was a person's default choice in the past, are there other ACTIONS they can choose? If hitting the wall is not what they want to choose these days, what is another action they can choose that will increase their peace? ____

____

____

____

____

____

____

When thinking about your own anger, can you imagine yourself ever being completely and totally peaceful and content with your life choices? Can you see yourself being peaceful even when others do negative things around you? ____

____

____

____

____

____

INCREASING MY PEACE – ACCOUNTABILITY BOX

DO YOU WANT CREDIT FOR THIS COURSE? REMEMBER TO KEEP TRACK OF YOUR DAILY STUDY BY COMPLETING THE INFORMATION BELOW TO GET YOUR CREDIT.

The month is______________; The day is ______________; The year is________; Solo study or group? __________

LIFE HAPPENS

It is generally believed that we hang around people who make us feel comfortable. It is generally believed that we avoid people who are different from us or who do not seem to communicate like we communicate.

In your opinion, how does hanging out with people just like you limit your growth or make it difficult to change? Is it possible to use your tools and make changes without changing who you feel comfortable hanging around? ____

____

____

____

If you slowly but surely change your anger level and increase your peace, what type of people do you think you will eventually hang around? ____________________________________

____

____

____

As a person ages, their friends are usually about the same age. As we get older, we like different things, we do different things, and we become very different than in our youth. Everyone changes, they just do it so slowly that they don't realize it. Can you think of things you did at 15 years of age that you simply do not do anymore? Can you think of yourself at 70 and the things you do today that will not be part of your daily life? ____________________________________

____

____

____

*How can you begin to use your GOGI Tools to start the process of a peaceful life now? Could you possibly encourage other people your age to mature into a peaceful life rather than to simply wait to grow old to learn how to be peaceful? What is your advice?*____________________________

____

____

____

____

____

____

INCREASING MY PEACE – ACCOUNTABILITY BOX

DO YOU WANT CREDIT FOR THIS COURSE? REMEMBER TO KEEP TRACK OF YOUR DAILY STUDY BY COMPLETING THE INFORMATION BELOW TO GET YOUR CREDIT.

The month is________________; The day is ______________; The year is________; Solo study or group? ____________

Day 3 – Anger Management vs. INCREASING YOUR PEACE

At GOGI, we would rather not have you manage your anger. We know that sounds funny, but we would rather have you increasing your internal peace so much that anger simply passes by without causing you any problems.

What does it mean in your life to think about anger in this way? Rather than "managing" your anger, does it make you want to increase your peace by using GOGI Tools instead? Write what you think about this concept and GOGI's approach at "Anger Management." ______________________

____

____

____

GOGI has been asked by many organizations and prisons to develop this "Anger Management" course. There seems to be a great need for something to address the high levels of anger and violence people experience. Many prisons state that the courses currently offered don't really help prisoners, that there is just as much violence as there always has been.

Why? Why is GOGI and why is this GOGI 'Course' different? ______________________

____

____

____

____

____

This course is coming to an end in a few days. If someone were to ask you what the best thing you got out of this course was, what would you say? ______________________

____

____

____

____

Would you recommend this course? Why or why not? ______________________

____

____

____

INCREASING MY PEACE – ACCOUNTABILITY BOX

DO YOU WANT CREDIT FOR THIS COURSE? REMEMBER TO KEEP TRACK OF YOUR DAILY STUDY BY COMPLETING THE INFORMATION BELOW TO GET YOUR CREDIT.

The month is________________; The day is ______________; The year is________; Solo study or group? __________

LIFE HAPPENS

Let's say you are sitting with four people with anger issues. Here are their issues. What tool do you suggest they each use and why?

Maria – *Sexually abused by family members. Started drinking and using drugs to feel better. Lost three kids to the system. Hates men. All men. Has no problem pushing or shoving anyone in her way. No one can hurt her. What tool and why?* ____

____

____

____

Kelvin – *Short and skinny and bullied badly as a kid. His only coping tool was to get really good at fist-fighting. He responds to anything and everything with aggression and violence. What tool and why?* ____

____

____

____

Officer Valdez – *Just plain angry at life. Doing time like the rest of the unhappy prisoners. What tool and why?* ____

____

____

____

____

Jose – *Walked from Guatemala to America only to get caught up in drugs and stealing. The better life he thought he was going to have has turned into a living hell every day and he wants to kill someone or kill himself all the time. What tool and why?* ______________________________________

____

____

____

____

____

____

DO YOU WANT CREDIT FOR THIS COURSE? REMEMBER TO KEEP TRACK OF YOUR DAILY STUDY BY COMPLETING THE INFORMATION BELOW TO GET YOUR CREDIT.

The month is________________; The day is ______________; The year is________; Solo study or group? ____________

Day 4 – WHAT IF YOU ARE THE SOLUTION?

In three days you will have successfully completed this course. The GOGI Tools were created BY and FOR prisoners. This course was based on their gifts to prisoners. What does that mean for you? It means that if you are a prisoner, you too can design something of value and importance. On this page you are to "design" your very own "Anger Management" course outline. Let's say it is a eight-week course given to angry prisoners who have gotten write-ups for violence.

List the subjects you would teach each week and why you chose that subject:

*Week 1 subject is:*____

*Why:*____

Week 2 subject is: ____

*Why:*____

Week 3 subject is: ____

*Why:*____

Week 4 subject is: ____

*Why:*____

Week 5 subject is: ____

*Why:*____

Week 6 subject is: ____

*Why:*____

Week 7 subject is: ____

*Why:*____

Week 8 subject is: ____

*Why:*____

Why do you think that teachers often learn more than their students when they teach? Could teaching this course help you learn more about your own levels of peace? How? ________________

____

____

____

____

INCREASING MY PEACE – ACCOUNTABILITY BOX

DO YOU WANT CREDIT FOR THIS COURSE? REMEMBER TO KEEP TRACK OF YOUR DAILY STUDY BY COMPLETING THE INFORMATION BELOW TO GET YOUR CREDIT.

The month is________________; The day is ______________; The year is_________; Solo study or group? ____________

LIFE HAPPENS

Let's say you have been given permission to teach your "Anger Management" course to a group of eight prisoners. Let's say all things are going well until management decides to shift Captains on your yard and the new Captain seems to be less agreeable with your peers meeting in the dayroom. While you are sitting in the dayroom, peacefully holding your class, the yard Lt. comes in and speaks with the officer of the day. You know something is up.

What do you tell your men? ____

____

The officer orders you "take it on home." What do you tell your men? ________________

____

____

The next day on the yard a few of your men start talking about how the system demands that they change but the cops won't let them. What do you tell your men? ________________

____

____

____

One of your guys simply can't let it go and he starts talking about taking out the cop that refuses to let the group meet.

What do you tell him? ____

____

____

What do you tell your men? ____

____

____

*You have become very peaceful through teaching this course and you come up with an idea that you can teach the course while on yard. You only have this idea because you have replaced your anger with a level of peace that permits you to find solutions. What do you tell your men?*____________

____

____

____

____

INCREASING MY PEACE – ACCOUNTABILITY BOX

DO YOU WANT CREDIT FOR THIS COURSE? REMEMBER TO KEEP TRACK OF YOUR DAILY STUDY BY COMPLETING THE INFORMATION BELOW TO GET YOUR CREDIT.

The month is_______________; The day is _______________; The year is_________; Solo study or group? _____________

Day 5 – LETTER OF CHANGE

You have two more days with this course. Today you get to write an outline of how YOU would create more PEACE on all prison yards. What would YOU do to permit PEACE to replace anger and violence?

I would do the following things to create more PEACE and have peace replace violence on the prison yards:

1) ____

2) ____

3) ____

Here are the types of officers I would hire:

4) ____

5) ____

6) ____

Here are the types of courses I would offer:

7) ____

8) ____

9) ____

Here is the type of leader I would be willing to become:

A leader who... ____

____

____

____

*I would also be a leader that...*____

____

____

I would be the example by... ____

____

____

____

INCREASING MY PEACE – ACCOUNTABILITY BOX

DO YOU WANT CREDIT FOR THIS COURSE? REMEMBER TO KEEP TRACK OF YOUR DAILY STUDY BY COMPLETING THE INFORMATION BELOW TO GET YOUR CREDIT.

The month is____________; The day is ____________; The year is________; Solo study or group? __________

LIFE HAPPENS

Let's say the corrections department gives you one full yard to "try" your way of doing corrections. Let's say you have 200 men on your yard. They give you the angriest and meanest and most disgruntled prisoners simply because they think you are going to fail.

What is the first thing you do?

While you are given this opportunity, you find out that your brother has been shot in a gang related drug deal gone bad. The rival gang is ON YOUR YARD and the brother of the guy who killed your little brother is TRAINING TO BE ONE OF YOUR Anger Management TEACHERS!

What do you do?

What tools do you use?

What is at stake in your decision?

How can you POSSIBLY be the solution when this big problem is staring you in the face?

INCREASING MY PEACE – ACCOUNTABILITY BOX

DO YOU WANT CREDIT FOR THIS COURSE? REMEMBER TO KEEP TRACK OF YOUR DAILY STUDY BY COMPLETING THE INFORMATION BELOW TO GET YOUR CREDIT.

The month is________________; The day is ______________; The year is________; Solo study or group? ____________

Day 6 – REAL CHOICES

GOGI understands that you have REAL choices to make and sometimes those choices are not as easy as choosing right from wrong. While choosing right from wrong sounds easy, there are often many other factors that go into every decision.

What do you think about the above statement? Does it fit with some of the decisions you have made?

GOGI also provides you with tools to begin to make more positive decisions, one at a time. We have learned that if a person makes slow and steady progress with their decisions that the difference between right and wrong becomes clearer and less convoluted.

What do you think about the above statement? Do you see how slowly practicing and applying the GOGI Tools can clear up the confusion in your decision-making?

The people who apply GOGI Tools to their entire lives state that they enjoy their lives more, feel they can give back to others, and sleep better without the need to use drugs or alcohol to make them feel better. Why might that be true for them?

What do you think about that claim? Do you think that something as simple as tools designed by and for prisoners could actually be a solid solution for your level of peace?

INCREASING MY PEACE – ACCOUNTABILITY BOX

DO YOU WANT CREDIT FOR THIS COURSE? REMEMBER TO KEEP TRACK OF YOUR DAILY STUDY BY COMPLETING THE INFORMATION BELOW TO GET YOUR CREDIT.

The month is__________________; The day is ______________; The year is________; Solo study or group? ____________

Day 7 – Recap and Review

What are the three TOOLS OF THE BODY?

1) ____

2) ____

3) ____

How is each tool used to increase peace?

1) ____

2) ____

3) ____

Who created the GOGI Tools? ______________________________

What is your opinion of how the GOGI Tools were created? ______________________

____

____

*Why do you think these tools might work for you in your life?*______________________

____

____

____

What in your past might have been different if you had the GOGI Tools? ______________

____

____

____

*What would you like to say to the prisoners who were brave enough to change their decisions, start living peaceful lives, use the GOGI Tools every day, and share those tools with others?*__________

____

____

____

____

____

INCREASING MY PEACE – ACCOUNTABILITY BOX

DO YOU WANT CREDIT FOR THIS COURSE? REMEMBER TO KEEP TRACK OF YOUR DAILY STUDY BY COMPLETING THE INFORMATION BELOW TO GET YOUR CREDIT.

The month is_______________; The day is _______________; The year is_________; Solo study or group? _____________

COURSE COMPLETION

INCREASING YOUR PEACE: Anger Management The GOGI Way Assessment

MAKE SURE YOU USE YOUR ENTIRE WORKBOOK AND FIND THE ANSWERS ON THOSE PAGES. THIS IS AN OPEN BOOK EVALUATION. THERE IS NO GRADE ASSIGNED.

Answer the following questions by writing in the space provided:

1. When you use the BOSS OF MY BRAIN tool, who is in charge of your emotions or anger?

____

2. What are the three parts of your brain you can choose to use with the BOSS OF MY BRAIN tool?

A)____

B)____

C)____

3. Who decides who the BOSS OF MY BRAIN is? _______________________

4. How does BELLY BREATHING help you increase your peace? _______________________

____

5. When could you use BELLY BREATHING to help you be more peaceful? _______________

____

6. What does the term loss aversion mean to you? How can BELLY BREATHING change your own thoughts about loss aversion? _______________________

____

7. Personally, when you use the FIVE SECOND LIGHTSWITCH tool, what can it help you prevent?____

____

8. One woman counted the names of her grandchildren and then went to a POSITIVE ACTION for her FIVE SECOND LIGHTSWITCH. If you could create your own reminder that you should be using the FIVE SECOND LIGHTSWITCH, what would it be? _______________________

____

9. How does OLD THOUGHT and NEW ACTION work with your FIVE SECOND LIGHTSWITCH tool? ____

____

INCREASING MY PEACE – ACCOUNTABILITY BOX

DO YOU WANT CREDIT FOR THIS COURSE? REMEMBER TO KEEP TRACK OF YOUR DAILY STUDY BY COMPLETING THE INFORMATION BELOW TO GET YOUR CREDIT.

The month is__________________; The day is ________________; The year is_________; Solo study or group? ______________

Complete the following sentences:

10. When I use BELLY BREATHING I can... ____

____

____

11. One way I can remind myself to use FIVE SECOND LIGHTSWITCH is... ____________________

____

____

12. When I am BOSS OF MY BRAIN, I am... ____

____

____

Circle the most appropriate answer:

13. I know I am using the BELLY BREATHING tool when I:

    a) close my eyes

    b) place one of my hands on my stomach and feel it move

    c) jump up and down

14. When I am BOSS OF MY BRAIN, I am choosing which part of my brain to use. I am most peaceful when I use:

    a) the OLD HABIT PART

    b) the part that controls my hearing

    c) the SMART PART

15. The FIVE SECOND LIGHTSWITCH is:

    a) a new way to multiply numbers

    b) a way to change your actions before acting on your anger

    c) something that can be installed in a home

The GOGI Calendar

GOGI TOOL STUDY SCHEDULE

JANUARY
Week 1 BOSS OF MY BRAIN
Week 2 BELLY BREATHING
Week 3 FIVE SECOND LIGHTSWITCH
Week 4 POSITIVE THOUGHTS
Week 5 REVIEW ABOVE

FEBRUARY
Week 1 POSITIVE WORDS
Week 2 POSITIVE ACTIONS
Week 3 CLAIM RESPONSIBILITY
Week 4 LET GO
Week 5 REVIEW ABOVE

MARCH
Week 1 FOR–GIVE
Week 2 WHAT IF
Week 3 REALITY CHECK
Week 4 ULTIMATE FREEDOM
Week 5 REVIEW ABOVE

APRIL
Week 1 BOSS OF MY BRAIN
Week 2 BELLY BREATHING
Week 3 FIVE SECOND LIGHTSWITCH
Week 4 POSITIVE THOUGHTS
Week 5 REVIEW ABOVE

MAY
Week 1 POSITIVE WORDS
Week 2 POSITIVE ACTIONS
Week 3 CLAIM RESPONSIBILITY
Week 4 LET GO
Week 5 REVIEW ABOVE

JUNE
Week 1 FOR–GIVE
Week 2 WHAT IF
Week 3 REALITY CHECK
Week 4 ULTIMATE FREEDOM
Week 5 REVIEW ABOVE

JULY
Week 1 BOSS OF MY BRAIN
Week 2 BELLY BREATHING
Week 3 FIVE SECOND LIGHTSWITCH
Week 4 POSITIVE THOUGHTS
Week 5 REVIEW ABOVE

AUGUST
Week 1 POSITIVE WORDS
Week 2 POSITIVE ACTIONS
Week 3 CLAIM RESPONSIBILITY
Week 4 LET GO
Week 5 REVIEW ABOVE

SEPTEMBER
Week 1 FOR–GIVE
Week 2 WHAT IF
Week 3 REALITY CHECK
Week 4 ULTIMATE FREEDOM
Week 5 REVIEW ABOVE

OCTOBER
Week 1 BOSS OF MY BRAIN
Week 2 BELLY BREATHING
Week 3 FIVE SECOND LIGHTSWITCH
Week 4 POSITIVE THOUGHTS
Week 5 REVIEW ABOVE

NOVEMBER
Week 1 POSITIVE WORDS
Week 2 POSITIVE ACTIONS
Week 3 CLAIM RESPONSIBILITY
Week 4 LET GO
Week 5 REVIEW ABOVE

DECEMBER
Week 1 FOR–GIVE
Week 2 WHAT IF
Week 3 REALITY CHECK
Week 4 ULTIMATE FREEDOM
Week 5 REVIEW ABOVE

The GOGI Tools for Positive Decision–Making and the Tool KEYWORDS

TOOLS OF THE BODY

BOSS OF MY BRAIN

THE THREE PARTS: the SMART part, the EMOTIONAL part, and the OLD HABIT part. Which one is the BOSS right now?

BELLY BREATHING

ONE HAND ON MY CHEST, ONE HAND ON MY BELLY. WHICH ONE IS MOVING RIGHT NOW? My brain works better when my belly moves.

FIVE SECOND LIGHTSWITCH

OLD THOUGHT → NEW ACTION. I have an OLD THOUGHT and I have a NEW ACTION

TOOLS OF CHOICE

POSITIVE THOUGHTS

The 3 Ps: Is it POWERFUL? Is it PRODUCTIVE? Is it POSITIVE?

POSITIVE WORDS

The 3 Ps: Is it POWERFUL? Is it PRODUCTIVE? Is it POSITIVE?

POSITIVE ACTIONS

The 3 Ps: Is it POWERFUL? Is it PRODUCTIVE? Is it POSITIVE?

TOOLS OF MOVING FORWARD

CLAIM RESPONSIBILITY

AM I PROUD OF THIS CHOICE? I am responsible for all my actions and all my reactions today.

LET GO

HAND/SQUASH/TOSS. When bothered, I put the feeling in my hand, squash it, and toss it away from me.

FOR–GIVE

FOR ME TO GIVE, I NEED DISTANCE FROM HARM. For me to give, I unhook from the past, and find my internal freedom.

TOOLS OF CREATION

WHAT IF?

WHAT IF I AM NOT MY PAST? No to the past = yes to the future.

REALITY CHECK

TEN AND TWO RULE – Ten steps forward and two steps back is still eight steps ahead.

ULTIMATE FREEDOM

BEING FREE IS UP TO ME. Being of service sets me internally free.

GOGI Pledge

May our commitment (group repeat)
To the study of GOGI (group repeat)
Grant us the joy (group repeat)
Of giving and receiving (group repeat)
So that our inner freedom (group repeat)
May be of maximum service (group repeat)
To those we love (group repeat)
And infinite others (group repeat)

I began the GOGI journey with Positive Thoughts. As we reached Positive Actions in week three, the words which stood out most were, "your reaction to disappointments and how you handle bad news, tells the world who you are." I got denied by board, so I can relate to this. Instead of reacting negatively the I'm used to, I applied this tool.

I'm learning to control my life. To me, this speaks volumns. I continue attending self-help and Education to futher better myself. Though everything starts with a thought, it's my Positive Actions that will define who I am. I know that actions have consequences, so the three keywords are helpful towards my decision making. So when in doubt, I remember to ask myself... Is this powerful? Is this productive? And is this positive?

This will play A pivotal role in the choices I make here on.

Francisca McGann
CSP Corcoran

Dearest GOGI Student,

The most important thing you could've learned in completing this INCREASING YOUR PEACE course is that anger is a choice.

It is NEVER your only choice.

Your life has been filled with experiences that drive your actions and your reactions. Honestly, in most cases, your actions and reactions have probably been pretty positive. In some cases, however, I'm certain you have regrets for the choices you have made.

The most exciting thing about the GOGI Tools For Positive Decision-Making is the fact that you own them and you can put them to use at any time, on any day, and in any circumstance. ANGER is a CHOICE, and so is the choice to INCREASE YOUR PEACE. You can always react and respond in a more powerful manner.

While some individuals mistakenly believe that anger shows power, in truth anger is our weakest response to everything.

An angry person may appear powerful, but they are really displaying the inability to handle things calmly. Angry people display their weakness for the world to see.

It is the peaceful person, the person who encourages harmony, that is the most powerful among us.

As you complete this course, and as you set this workbook aside, please do not forget the option you have to be a powerful, productive, and positive human being from this day forward.

With Love,

Coach Taylor

INCREASING MY PEACE – ACCOUNTABILITY BOX

DO YOU WANT CREDIT FOR THIS COURSE? REMEMBER TO KEEP TRACK OF YOUR DAILY STUDY BY COMPLETING THE INFORMATION BELOW TO GET YOUR CREDIT.

The month is_________________; The day is _______________; The year is________; Solo study or group? ____________

DO YOU KNOW YOUR GOGI?

You know your GOGI if you can answer the following questions. These questions are provided to GOGI by students contacting GOGI after their successful Board hearings. They state the Board asked these questions during their interviews.

- **What are the four sections GOGI TOOLS?**

  1) TOOLS OF THE BODY
  2) TOOLS OF CHOICE
  3) TOOLS OF MOVING FORWARD
  4) TOOLS OF CREATION

- **What are the names of the GOGI Tools?**

  BOSS OF MY BRAIN, BELLY BREATHING, FIVE SECOND LIGHTSWITCH, POSITIVE THOUGHTS, POSITIVE WORDS, POSITIVE ACTIONS, CLAIM RESPONSIBILITY, LET GO, FOR–GIVE, WHAT IF, REALITY CHECK, ULTIMATE FREEDOM

- **Who created the GOGI Tools and who created GOGI?**

  Prisoners created the GOGI Tools to share with other prisoners. All GOGI materials were given to GOGI by prisoners.

- **What is the GOGI Pledge and who created it?**

  A prisoner created the GOGI Pledge to unite all students learning GOGI so together they could make their communities better places to live.

May our commitment (repeat)
To the study of GOGI (repeat)
Grant us the joy (repeat)
Of giving and receiving (repeat)
So that our inner freedom (repeat)
May be of maximum service (repeat)
To those we love (repeat)
And infinite others (repeat)

- **Why does GOGI have a calendar?**

  GOGI students study according to the GOGI Calendar because when all of GOGI studies according to the GOGI Calendar, no person will ever be alone in their GOGI studies. Each week of the year we focus on a different GOGI Tool.

INCREASING MY PEACE – ACCOUNTABILITY BOX

DO YOU WANT CREDIT FOR THIS COURSE? REMEMBER TO KEEP TRACK OF YOUR DAILY STUDY BY COMPLETING THE INFORMATION BELOW TO GET YOUR CREDIT.

The month is________________; The day is ______________; The year is________; Solo study or group? ____________

- **Why is GOGI Group study coordinated with the calendar?**

  So all students of GOGI everywhere are united in the study of our tools.

- **Who created, and why does GOGI have an official meeting format?**

  Prisoners with experience in many different types of group meetings created the official meeting format. It is used so all GOGI meetings follow a uniform format that is familiar to anyone attending meetings in different locations.

- **What are the Keywords each of the TOOLS?**

TOOLS OF THE BODY

BOSS OF MY BRAIN: THE THREE PARTS: There are three parts that matter: SMART PART, EMOTIONAL PART, and the OLD HABIT PART. Which one is the boss right now?

BELLY BREATHING: ONE HAND ON MY CHEST, ONE HAND ON MY BELLY. WHICH ONE IS MOVING RIGHT NOW? My brain works better when my belly moves.

FIVE SECOND LIGHTSWITCH: OLD THOUGHT → NEW ACTION. I have an OLD THOUGHT and I have a NEW ACTION.

TOOLS OF CHOICE

POSITIVE THOUGHTS: Is it Powerful? Productive? Positive?

POSITIVE WORDS: Is it Powerful? Productive? Positive?

POSITIVE ACTIONS: Is it Powerful? Productive? Positive?

TOOLS OF MOVING FORWARD

CLAIM RESPONSIBILITY: AM I PROUD OF THIS CHOICE? I am responsible for all my actions and all my reactions today.

LET GO: HAND/SQUASH/TOSS. When bothered, I put the feeling in my hand, squash it, and toss it away from me.

FOR–GIVE: FOR ME TO GIVE, I NEED DISTANCE FROM HARM. For me to give, I unhook from the past, and find my internal freedom.

TOOLS OF CREATION

WHAT IF: WHAT IF I AM NOT MY PAST? No to the past = yes to the future.

REALITY CHECK: TEN AND TWO RULE. Ten steps forward and two steps back is still eight steps ahead.

ULTIMATE FREEDOM: BEING FREE IS UP TO ME. Living a life of service gives me ULTIMATE FREEDOM.

GOGI relies on input from students to direct our growth. On the following pages you have an opportunity to let your voice be heard by GOGI. Please gently tear out and send us any pages you wish to share from the following section.

Send to: GOGI Education PO Box 2274 Mesquite, NV, USA 89024

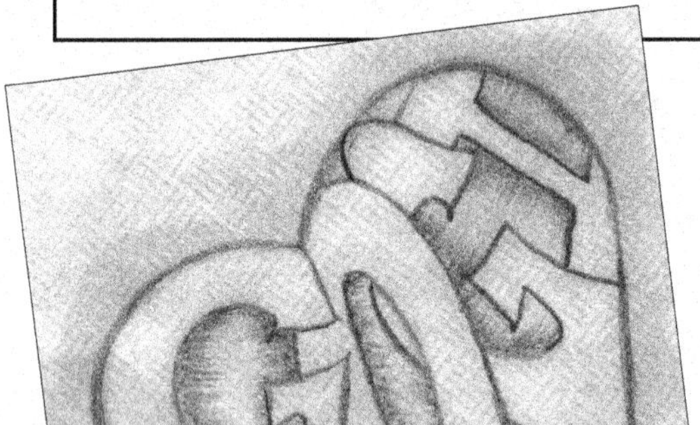

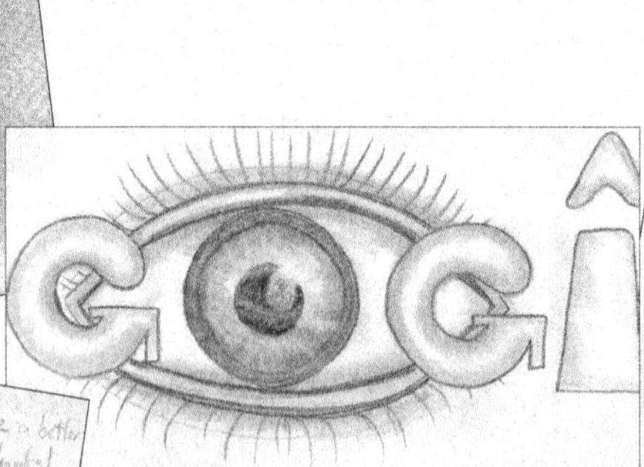

My Gift to GOGI ~ my art, poem, or activity

My signature______________________________ ID number ______________Location ________________

Print your name______________________________

Mail your gift to GOGI at: GOGI Education, Gifts to GOGI, PO Box 2274, Mesquite, NV 89024

My Gift to GOGI ~ my art, poem, or activity

My signature______________________________ ID number ______________Location ________________

Print your name______________________________

Mail your gift to GOGI at: GOGI Education, Gifts to GOGI, PO Box 2274, Mesquite, NV 89024

TEAR HERE AND MAIL TO GOGI

My Gift to GOGI ~ a letter I have not written

In all our lives there are words we do not say, letters we do not write. In this space, you can write a letter you might be unable to send, but you can share with others your thoughts and feelings. What would you say in your letter?

Dear ________________________________

Respectfully,

My name is: ________________________________

My ID number is: ________________________________

My Address is: ________________________________

TEAR HERE AND MAIL TO GOGI

Mail your gift to GOGI at: GOGI Education, Gifts to GOGI, PO Box 2274, Mesquite, NV 89024

My Gift to GOGI ~ letter to a young person

Write what you wish someone would have told you, or what you would like to share with a young person who may be headed down the wrong path. What would you like to say to encourage them to make positive decisions?

Dear Young Person,____________________________________

Respectfully,

My name is: ____________________________________

My ID number is: ____________________________________

My Address is: ____________________________________

Mail your gift to GOGI at: GOGI Education, Gifts to GOGI, PO Box 2274, Mesquite, NV 89024

Let Your GOGI Voice be Heard! Write a Letter to Your Governor.

This is your opportunity to let your voice be heard by your state's Governor. Tell them why you love GOGI and what you have learned from your GOGI studies. Help them to understand how GOGI's positive culture is changing lives, including yours.

Dear Governor,

____

____

____

____

____

____

____

____

____

____

____

____

____

____

____

Respectfully,

My name is: ______________________________

My ID number is: ___________________________

My Address is: _____________________________

____

TEAR HERE AND MAIL TO GOGI